THE WORLD'S BEST
DRINKS
WHERE TO FIND THEM
& HOW TO MAKE THEM

CONTENTS

FOREWORD

BY VICTORIA MOORE

Smell is the most evocative sense we have. One sniff of a glass filled with thick yoghurt mixed with luscious Alphonso mango can be enough to conjure up the chaotic hum of an Indian street – the flashes of colours, jangle of horns, wood smoke, drains, the beggars, the dirt, the cries and the calls. In the same way, the sugar-drenched sourness of a caipirinha can saturate your mind with Brazilian sun and a glass of spicy *glögi* transport you to the pine forests of a Nordic midwinter.

The part of the brain responsible for this potent effect is called the olfactory cortex. It's here that associations are made between the input coming from the flavour receptors in our nose and the memory traces from earlier experiences of that drink. The olfactory cortex possesses an almost magical ability to reconstruct a whole from a small fragment. In the same way that when we hear the timbre of a loved one's voice, their whole being seems to enter the room, the tiniest sip of a drink can connect us to a vast tapestry of remembered emotions, vistas and sensations.

The more we travel, the richer this experience becomes, of course, and perhaps that's one reason why our appetite for different drinks has become more adventurous. We don't always need to have been to a place to have a sense of it, either. Memories can also be built from films, photographs and snatches of music played on a sunny afternoon.

This Lonely Planet book of the world's best drinks is not, then, a mere drink guide, offering a brief guide to wine, charting the rise of artisan tonic water; steering you through the different styles of beer, from blonde ale to witbier to dunkel and providing a pithy history of the planet's most famous spirits. It is also a travelogue that will take you to the sophisticated and chic gallerias of Milan where you can sip negronis made with carmine-coloured Campari as well as venturing into less well-trammelled territories. In these pages you might make new discoveries such as the *terremoto* – a Chilean cocktail made using pineapple ice cream, white wine and grenadine and apparently created in 1985 shortly after the earthquake that shook Valparaiso. And did you know that the Paloma – made with tequila, grapefruit juice and soda – is more widely drunk in Mexico than the Margarita? I didn't.

Sophisticated favourites like the Martini sit alongside the *tongba* - Himalayan millet beer quite possibly known only to trekkers who will associate it with the smell of a yak-dung fire and the relief of resting aching legs.

This book isn't only about booze either – it promises to expand your non-alcoholic repertoire with *horchata* from Mexico and East African cardamom tea, as well as reminding you of that old favourite, the fiery-sweet root beer float.

It only remains for me to say cheers – and, of course, happy travelling.

© TIM E EWING

© TIM E WHITE

BEER

Gone are the days when the only choice you faced when ordering a beer was whether you wanted a pint or a half. Today you can get your beer aged in barrels or fermented with cherries, blended with wine, flavoured with herbs, or unadulterated, with the beverage's four core ingredients speaking for themselves. With just malt, hops, water and yeast, brewers can conjure up natural flavours of caramel and toast, chocolate and coffee, citrus, banana, pine trees and cloves. Whether you opt for a bottle of rose petal-infused stout or a more traditional pint of pale ale, there's nothing quite like settling down in an unpretentious pub with a froth-topped pint in hand. →

HISTORY

The origins of beer are as murky as those early pints would have been. Long-attributed to the Egyptians, it is now thought that the first beers were drunk in Mesopotamia – modern-day Iraq – almost 4000 years ago. One thing that is agreed on is that the recipe for beer happened by accident, perhaps when a failed batch of bread fermented, providing its eaters with a buzz that their sandwiches didn't normally deliver. Those thick, opaque brews gradually evolved into the clear beers we drink today, although beers akin to the first brews are still sipped in some parts, like *umqombothi* in South Africa or the Nepalese *tongba*.

TASTING

Beer tends to be overlooked by gourmands – considered a drink to swill, rather than sniff. But beer can, and should, be tasted in just the same way as wine. Look first for hop aromas, which can range from Europe's earthy, spiced notes to the in-your-face pine needles and passion fruit that American hops offer up. On second sniffing, seek out the malt – think toast, toffee, biscuit and chocolate. Taste-wise, beers range from dessert-sweet to mouth-dryingly bitter, depending on the alcohol content and amount of hops added. No need to swirl before you sip – you don't want to kill the carbonation. Oh, and beer tasting never involves spitting!

VARIANTS

Although the sub-styles are plentiful, there are just two main branches of the beer family – lager and ale. The difference boils down to the yeast used – ales ferment at warmer temperatures, while the yeast used to create lager prefers things a little cooler. The many sub-strains of yeast all come with their own flavour profiles but, broadly speaking, ales tend to be fruitier, a little more complex and aren't served so cold (8–14°C). Lagers are generally crisper and served cooler, though ice-cold fridges should be reserved for beer whose flavours you want to mask – anything below 4°C is simply too cold to taste.

DID YOU KNOW?

● A pint of standard lager has more calories than a pint of dry stout.

● If the head (foam) on your beer disappears without trace, there might be soap remnants on the glass.

● In Belgium every single beer has its own dedicated glass, designed to best show off the aromas and flavours of each brew.

ALE

When picturing an ale, most people think of something copper-coloured and roasty, but the gamut covers everything from light, easy-drinking blonde ales and refreshing wheat beers to hoppy IPAs, chocolatey stouts and rich Belgian styles boasting toffee-like tones. The American Beer Judge Certification Program (BJCP) recognises over 120 styles of beer, though you won't find all of them on the average pub chalkboard. Try these common ones, listed in recommended tasting order.

BLONDE ALE

A light, malty style providing a nice leap from lager to ale. Try it with fried fish or a light chicken dish.

WEISSBIER

Expect notes of banana, bread and cloves from this German-style brew which is usually unfiltered and hazy. Try it with goats' cheese or banoffee pie.

WITBIER

This Belgian beer comes with added orange peel and coriander, lending a refreshing, perfumed taste. It's an excellent breakfast beer.

TIPS FOR TASTING

● When pairing ales with food, carbonation and body are as important as flavour. Beers with plenty of bubbles work well with rich foods, and when it comes to body match like with like – a delicate witbier will complement sushi, while a heavy stout is a dream with steak.

● As with wine, beers are usually tasted in order of intensity and while colour is a fair indicator, moving from light to dark doesn't always work. Hoppy styles – like American IPA – come with an intense bitterness and are best sampled after something darker but less potent, like a dry stout.

● Flavour-wise, look for harmonies – the roasted, toasty elements in malty beers pair well with foods that echo these flavours – think caramelised ribs or chargrilled meats. Hops have the ability to cut through rich or fatty dishes, but will accentuate the heat in spicy fare.

PALE ALE
English versions are malt-forward while American Pale Ales are more about the hops. Try it with meat pie or a toffee-themed dessert.

STOUT
A dark beer that can be sweet or dry, with notes of coffee and chocolate. Try it with a hearty beef stew or a slab of chocolate.

INDIA PALE ALE (IPA)
American IPAs offer full-on floral, fruity aromas and a long, bitter finish. English IPAs are more subtle and slightly lower in alcohol. Try with strong cheese like Gruyère or Gorgonzola.

LAGER

When it comes to lager, there's usually only one image on people's minds – a pint of clear, golden liquid whose bubbles rise to form a frothy white head. Sure, pale lager is still the most popular beer style, with estimates suggesting that around 90% of all beer consumed worldwide fits into this category. But the likes of Budweiser, Tsingtao or Fosters are not the only members of the lager family.

PALE LAGER
The world's most popular style is crisp and refreshing without any overpowering flavours. Try it with fried chicken or a salad.

PILSNER
Dark gold in colour, pilsners have a more pronounced bitterness and a sturdy malt backbone. Try with spicy dishes like jambalaya or curry.

DUNKEL
A dark lager filled with aromas – and flavours – of nuts, toast, toffee and chocolate. Try it with pulled pork or pecan pie.

TIPS FOR TASTING

Although the world's strongest lager, an eisbock from Germany, weighs in at a whopping 57% ABV, in general, lagers tend to be lighter and more subtle in flavour than ales. That's not to say that they don't pair well with food though – pilsners in particular are a great partner for many dishes, thanks to their full-flavoured balance of malt and hops.

BOCK

These rich lagers come in numerous guises, ranging from 6–14% ABV. Look out for toffee, caramel and toast flavours. Try with a sticky toffee pudding or roast duck.

● *by Lucy Corne*

ORIGINS

No one can say for certain who invented the michelada. Mi-chel-ada most likely is an abbreviated form of the Spanish phrase 'mi chela helada' ('my ice-cold brew'). The drink has long been popular along the Pacific coast and in major cities such as Mexico City and Guadalajara, but you can find it pretty much anywhere in Mexico nowadays.

MEXICO

MICHELADA

The michelada is the preferred Mexican brunch drink and with good reason: the refreshing beer cocktail goes down oh-so-nicely with spicy food, and yes, it even calms those throbbing hangovers.

YOU'LL NEED

2 tbsp coarse salt
1 tbsp chilli powder, preferably Tajín brand
1¼ limes
350ml (12fl oz) Mexican beer (light or dark)
2 dashes Worcestershire sauce
1 dash Maggi sauce
2 dashes hot sauce, preferably Tabasco
3–4 cubes of ice

METHOD

1 Mix the salt and chilli powder seasoning on a plate.

2 Cut the whole lime in half and rub it around the rim of a chilled 475ml (16fl oz) beer mug or large glass.

3 Upend the glass and dip the edge in the salt and chilli powder mixture, so the edge is coated in the powder.

4 Pour cold beer into the glass, taking care not to disturb the prepared rim.

5 Squeeze the whole lime.

6 Add the lime juice, Worcestershire, Maggi and Tabasco sauces to the glass.

7 Stir and add ice if desired.

8 Garnish with the reserved lime quarter by positioning it on the rim of the glass.

TASTING NOTES

When ordering a michelada in Mexico, a waiter might ask if you prefer 'clara o oscura' (light or dark) beer. Don't worry, there's no wrong answer. Mexican beers Bohemia, Negra Modelo and Pacífico work particularly well.

A spicy michelada is often referred to as a Cubana. Similar to a Bloody Mary, sans vodka, the Cubana's hot sauce and chilli powder help you sweat out those party toxins, creating the perfect hangover remedy. Nothing beats knocking back micheladas in a boisterous *cantina*, where you can bond with locals while watching televised *fútbol* matches, get slap-happy playing dominoes or chow down bar grub. ● *by Phillip Tang*

TASTING NOTES
The World's Best Drinks

CIDER

Cider, the fermented juice of apples, is enjoying a booming renaissance in the 21st century. Given its qualities – from crisp to cloudy, mellowing to invigorating – it's hard to see why it ever fell out of favour. For 2000 years it's inspired devotion and thirst, spreading from its heartland of Northern France and Southern England to become the summer tipple of choice for many. →

TASTING

Ciders range from very sweet to mouth-puckeringly dry, from clear and fizzy to murky and still. The final taste depends on the blend: more than 365 cider cultivars are known, classified as sweet (such as the Sweet Coppin); bittersweet (Brown Snout, Dabinett); sharp (Bramley's Seedling, Crimson King); or bittersharp (Stoke Red, Fox Whelp).

After scratting (crushing), the must (juice) is fermented. Sweetness and alcohol levels depend on filtration and length of fermentation (longer equals boozier).

Good cider deserves the same careful appreciation as good beer and wine. Served at the right temperature (lightly chilled) in the right glass (pints for English ciders; wine glasses for its continental cousins) it's excellent on its own, or with food. Match it like white wine: sweet with sweet and spicy foods; dry and acidic with fatty foods.

HISTORY

The discovery that the sugar in apples could be converted into alcohol must have come soon after the fruit's first cultivation, which was in full swing in Mesopotamia by 1500BC. Julius Caesar found it drunk by the Celts of Kent and Normandy in 55BC, and the post-1066 Normans ensured its popularity grew. French and English colonists carried it to North America where – until the introduction of German beer-making techniques – it was the most popular tipple. After a lull in the 20th century, it's come fizzing back into fashion.

DID YOU KNOW?

● Spanish *sidra* is traditionally 'thrown' (poured from the height of a metre) to enhance flavour.

● In 14th-century England, children were purportedly baptised in cider.

● War with wine-supplying nations (principally France and Spain) usually resulted in a spike in demand for English cider.

VARIANTS

French *cidre*, from Normandy and Brittany, tends to be sparkling, deeply-coloured and dry-to-quite sweet. Spanish *sidra*, from Asturias and the Basque country, is more often still and musty, with a yeasty flavour and slight vinegary tang. Bottled and consumed like wine, and subject to strict controls, *cidre* and *sidra* don't come mass-produced, or cheap. British ciders, predominantly from the West country, can be clear and sparkling, or murky unfiltered 'scrumpy' with a higher alcohol content and a hint of orchard humus. New World cidermakers incorporate all three European traditions, so ciders from the US, Canada and Australia might sit anywhere on the spectrum.

Perry – cider made from pears – is a closely-related drink. ● *by Hugh McNaughton*

ORIGINS

Mulled cider has its origins in a drink called *wassail*, a warm beverage popular in cider-producing counties in south-west England during medieval times. Orchard 'wassailing', aka wailings bestowing good health upon cider apple trees, was traditionally held on 17 January, the 12th night of the Julian calendar. The objective? Scare away evil spirits to ensure a good apple harvest the following year. The king and queen wassailers would lead a procession to a tree where the queen was lifted up to place her toast dunked in wassail as a gift to the tree spirits.

UNITED KINGDOM

MULLED CIDER

SERVES 10

Oh, the scent of warm apples, with layers of sweet spice and a rich slug of brandy – once you've smelt this cider brewing, you'll never imagine a winter without it.

YOU'LL NEED

2l (3½ pt) cider (best quality you can find)
2 oranges: 1 juiced, the other sliced
6 cloves
2 cinnamon sticks
2 tsp brandy
4–5 tsp soft dark brown sugar/honey (optional)

METHOD

1 Pour the cider into a large pan on low heat and let it warm for a few minutes.

2 Juice one of the oranges.

3 Add the orange juice, cloves and cinnamon sticks to the pan, then slowly turn up the heat until the liquid is close to boiling point.

4 When almost boiling, reduce the heat to a simmer – this is where you 'mull' it – for 10 to 20 minutes.

5 Take the pan off the heat, add the brandy and sliced orange.

6 Stir and taste, adding sugar/honey if you'd prefer a sweeter mixture.

7 Ladle into mugs and serve to lucky friends, preferably around a fire.

TASTING NOTES

It's threatening to snow. Weaving around wellington-clad revellers at the little English village fete, Christmas lights strobing through the looming fog, you can't feel your nose and the icy wind long ago rendered your gloves ineffective. A steamy waft of warm apple suddenly billows in from a stall where a vat of amber brew, dotted with cloves, cinnamon and orange slices, bubbles enticingly. Take the mug you're offered: this is the perfect antidote to a bitter winter's eve. With any luck, your cider is made the traditional way – layering apples and straw in a cider press – adding an extra zing and fruitiness to the rich, sweet spices that develop during the mulling process. The brandy kicks in steadily, soothingly. Another please. ● *by Karyn Noble*

TASTING NOTES
The World's Best Drinks

WINE

A complex fruit drink made from fermented grapes, wine is one of the world's most popular tipples, consumed on a wide range of occasions in every conceivable location. Often vaunted for its antioxidants and other health-related benefits, its most immediate effect is stress-relief and promotion of a party mood, encouraged by an alcohol content of 9–15 per cent. It also has a synergistic relationship with food, both as a digestive aid and complementary partner to particular ingredients. →

HISTORY

Archaeological evidence dates winemaking back to Georgia, around 8000 years ago. Much later, around 1100BC, it trickled west into Italy, Spain and France as the Phoenicians began trading across the Mediterranean. The Greeks and then Romans developed such a serious appetite for the stuff that they each rustled up a wine god (Dionysus and Bacchus) and planted great swathes of vines across Europe.

Wine spread around the world from the 16th century, with conquistadors, traders, missionaries and migrants planting grapes wherever they would grow. The advent of the tightly-corked glass bottle in the 17th century was a particular watershed, making wine easier to store, preserve and transport.

While 'Old World' producers from Europe still dominate production, the 'New World' is on the charge, led by Australia, New Zealand, South Africa, the US and South America.

TASTING

There are more than 1000 grape varieties and myriad winemaking techniques, resulting in an almost endless array of flavours spread across spectrums of sweetness, acidity, mouth-feel and aroma.

To optimise flavours, serve it at the right temperature – generally 13–15°C for reds, 8–12°C for whites. Holding your glass up to the light to assess colour and clarity has no bearing on flavour, but will make you look smart. Give it a good sniff, then a swirl, then another sniff to hoover up the aromas. Then taste the wine, rolling it around your taste buds for a few moments before swallowing.

So, how is it? Flamboyant, grippy, austere, steely, *pétillant*? If words fail you, find a cheat sheet such as the Wine Aroma Wheel to help you pick the plums in Pinot Noir and the violets in Viognier.

DID YOU KNOW?

Industrial production and increasing grape yields mean that more wine is produced than actually drunk. Many countries have experienced a 'wine glut', with rumours of Sauvignon Blanc being poured down drains in the dead of night to avoid scaring the horses. The French once resorted to 'emergency distillation' of excess wine into ethanol to be used in petrol. Bacchus and Dionysus must have wept.

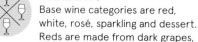

VARIANTS

Base wine categories are red, white, rosé, sparkling and dessert. Reds are made from dark grapes, with the skin pigments providing colour. White wines can be made from white or dark grapes. Rosé's pink tinge comes from dark grape skins used to colour the juice briefly. Dessert wines are made from deliciously wizened fruit with higher sugar content.

A range of flavours can be found even within each varietal. This is due to *terroir* – the unique combination of geography, geology and climate in which they're grown. South Australia's warmth produces lush, jammy Syrah (also known as Shiraz), while the same varietal from the cooler Rhône Valley in France will be leaner and more peppery.

Then there's blending, the purposes of which are to achieve consistency, round out rough edges and add depth or complexity. Blending occurs mainly with reds.

RED WINE

There are dozens of commonly consumed red wines, some made from a single grape variety and others from blends. Those dominating shop shelves include Cabernet Sauvignon, Merlot, Pinot Noir, Syrah, Zinfandel and Tempranillo.

Generally, tannins from grape skins give red wines a dryer, more astringent taste than whites, and they help the wine age. Indeed, many reds cellar particularly well. Flavours range wildly, from red cherries and the forest floor funk of silky Pinot Noir, to blackcurrant and pepper in a savoury Syrah.

Reds are predominantly consumed with food. Cabernet Sauvignon and lamb dance together like Fred and Ginger, while Merlot's mild nature suits all sorts of dishes including roast chicken and spaghetti bolognese. Reds like to breathe, so are best served in a wide, bowl-like glass.

WHITE WINE

White wines are more often produced in pure varietal form. Popular grapes include Sauvignon Blanc, Chardonnay, Riesling, Pinot Gris (also known as Pinot Grigio), Chenin Blanc and Gewürztraminer.

Whites are more delicate than reds, often with pronounced fresh fruit notes. Gooseberry and passion fruit are typical of Sauvignon Blanc, peach and vanilla in Chardonnay, and lemony zing in Pinot Gris. Glasses with a small opening help to retain crisp clean characters by reducing oxidation.

Such delicate flavours are best appreciated alongside subtle-tasting food such as fish and salads. Sweeter, aromatic styles such as Riesling and Gewürztraminer, however, are the perfect foil for a spicy Thai curry. Lighter whites are often enjoyed as refreshment or an aperitif, with a strawberryish rosé a particular favourite on a summery afternoon.

SPARKLING WINE

Sparkling wines can be made from any grape, with secondary fermentation accounting for the bubbles of carbon dioxide. The most famous fizz is from Champagne, made only with Chardonnay, Pinot Noir or Petit Meunier. The New World version – called *méthode traditionelle* because it can't be called Champagne – emulates the French with similar grapes and techniques. Other nations, however, put their own spin on things, with the Spanish producing Cava from their traditional Macabeu, Parellada and Xarel·lo grapes, and the Italians making Prosecco from Glera.

Sparkling wines range from fresh and fruity to rich and complex, often redolent of apples, brioche or toasted nuts. Traditionally uncorked as a celebratory treat, 'bubbles' are now so ubiquitous they're often sipped as an aperitif and quaffed in cocktails. Pair a truly great bottle with oysters *au naturel*. And always serve your fizz in a tall 'flute' to stop it from falling flat.

CHAMPAGNE

DESSERT WINE

Dessert wines can be made from various grapes harvested late when sugar levels are high. Noble rot – which surfaces when moisture levels are just right – is the dessert winemaker's friend, as is the touch of frost that results in 'ice wine'. Volumes are generally small and therefore precious.

Colloquially called 'stickies', dessert wines are relatively viscous. Their concentrated, perfumed flavours such as honey, apricot and pineapple are best savoured from a small wine glass. Serving them too cold deadens the flavour and is therefore a cardinal sin.

Delectable late harvest wine matches include Riesling with blue cheese, and Sauternes with crème brûlée. ● *by Lee Slater*

ORIGINS

Warm, spiced wine made its first appearance in the records almost 2000 years ago, starting in Rome and making its way north. The drink became popular along the Rhine, through Germany and into the chilly Alps. The inviting smell wafted slowly north, where the cosy, wintertime drink has taken on a life of its own. We especially like the Finnish variety. Extra shot of vodka? Don't mind if we do.

FINLAND

GLÖGI

In the Nordic countries where spices were once as rare as a warm December evening, the imported tradition of hot mulled wine quickly became a Christmas and midwinter staple.

YOU'LL NEED

750ml (25fl oz) red wine

1l (34fl oz) blackcurrant or red grape juice (or a mixture of both)

white granulated sugar, to taste (up to 100g/4oz if desired)

2 cinnamon sticks

½ vanilla pod

4 whole cloves

4 cardamom pods

1 tsp ground candied orange peel (or zest from 1 orange)

1 tbsp raisins

1 tbsp blanched slivered almonds

vodka, to taste

METHOD

1 Place the wine and juice in a large pan over a medium heat until almost boiling. For a virgin version, leave out the wine (and vodka) and double the juice.

2 Add the sugar and dissolve fully. Bring down the heat.

3 Add all the spices (for easy straining tie them up in cheesecloth).

4 Simmer for at least one hour on a low heat (or up to several hours).

5 Remove spice bag or strain out spices.

6 Pour into glasses, dropping a few raisins and almonds into each glass.

7 Add vodka to taste.

TASTING NOTES

Hot wine, mulled in exotic spices with a generous helping of vodka; what's not to love? Known as *glögi* in Finland and *glögg* in Sweden, you can buy it ready-made in alcoholic or non-alcoholic varieties, particularly from a certain well-known Scandinavian furniture store. In Finland, the homemade tradition is back in vogue: there are few greater pleasures on a day that gets dark just after lunch than the smell of vanilla, cloves, cinnamon and wine filling up a home. Families often have a non-alcoholic version using blackcurrant or apple juice. *Glögi* is typically served with gingerbread cookies. ● *by Alex Leviton*

ORIGINS

Originally known as a *Rioja Libre* or *Cuba Libre del pobre* (poor man's Cuba Libre) in 1970s Spain, its current name was later coined at a Basque festival. According to legend, its creators realised they were serving bad wine and decided to disguise the taste by mixing it with Coke; the drink became an unlikely hit. Named after their two friends, Kalimero and Motxo, it's popular throughout Spain and is an icon of Basque culture.

SERVES 8

SPAIN

KALIMOTXO

Guaranteed to have wine purists up in arms, this cheeky beverage is a mix of red wine and cola. It's refreshing, cheap and championed by many – especially Spanish teenagers.

YOU'LL NEED
1l (32fl oz) red wine
(preferably strong and dry,
of the cheaper variety)
1l (32fl oz) cola
Ice
Slice of lemon (optional)

METHOD
1 Mix equal parts of the red wine and cola. Serve with ice.

(If you want to spice up this simple drink you could add a slice of lemon, but *kalimotxo* purists – if they even exist – may disagree.)

TASTING NOTES
Some may have doubts about this drink, especially given its reputation as the drink of choice for Spanish teenagers; they are known for buying the harshest of wines and swishing it together with Coca-Cola in a plastic bag at *botellones* (impromptu street gatherings). However, on a sizzling summer night, surrounded by a boisterous crowd at a Spanish festival, it all starts to make sense. Like the festival itself, the drink is cheerful and unfussy. It comes in a plastic glass loaded with ice. For a few euros it's immediately satisfying. The sugar and caffeine pep you up, but are balanced by the mellowing effect of the wine. How else are you expected to last well into the next morning? ● *by Stephanie Ong*

ORIGINS

Named for the golden Australian flower reputedly introduced to Europe by British explorer Captain Cook, the first mimosa was purportedly served at The Ritz, Paris in 1925 by head barman Frank Meier. However, the recipe may have been pilfered from London's Buck's Club, at which the first Buck's Fizz (which uses the same ingredients but with a higher ratio of orange juice) was poured in 1921. Whatever its true origin, the fact remains that, in the words of the Duke of Edinburgh, 'Champagne and orange juice is a great drink.'

SERVES 1

PARIS, FRANCE

MIMOSA

Simple yet undeniably chic, this classic breakfast cocktail seamlessly transforms the morning meal into a bona fide event.

YOU'LL NEED

40ml (1½fl oz) freshly-squeezed orange juice (or fresh blood orange juice for a zesty alternative)

15ml (½fl oz) Grand Marnier or a dash of orange bitters (optional)

120ml (4fl oz) Brut Champagne or dry sparkling wine

METHOD

1 Add orange juice and, if using, Grand Marnier or bitters, to a champagne flute.

2 Top with Champagne or sparkling wine.

TASTING NOTES

Solving the age-old crisis of what to order when it's perhaps a little too early in the day for a Champagne toast, but too special an occasion not to make one, the mimosa has rightly earned its title as the queen of chic boozy breakfast beverages. The hue of morning sunshine, this simple yet sophisticated tipple balances a sweet vitamin C hit with carbonated pep to provide the ultimate wake-up call. Word has it director Alfred Hitchcock was responsible for introducing the mimosa as a US weekend brunch staple in the 1940s, and to this day, few can deny that Sunday is as important an occasion as any to warrant a mimosa toast – wherever in the world one is breakfasting. ● *by Sarah Reid*

ORIGINS

Sangria has a history in Spain that stretches back to the Romans who are recorded enjoying a tipple of watered-down red wine with fruit back in the 4th century; water was deemed unsafe to drink unless combined with alcohol to kill off any bacteria. The name comes from *sangre* (blood) due to its ruby red colour. Sangria was famously introduced to the USA in the Spanish Pavilion during the 1964 New York World's Fair.

SERVES 4

SPAIN

SANGRIA

Sangria is a refreshing summer drink based on full-bodied red wine, spiked with liquor and combined with fruit (juice and wedges), sugar and soda water or lemonade.

YOU'LL NEED

1 bottle (24fl oz) of dry, full-bodied red wine, preferably Spanish

2 tbsp orange juice

3 tbsp orange liqueur, such as Gran Torres

1 tbsp sugar

1 orange, thinly sliced (diced peach or apple may also be added)

1 lemon, thinly sliced

250ml (8½fl oz) soda water, sparkling water or *gaseosa* (the Spanish soda equivalent)

ice cubes

METHOD

1 Combine all the ingredients in a large jug except for the soda water.

2 Cover and refrigerate for several hours or overnight.

3 Add the soda and ice cubes and serve immediately in goblet-sized wine glasses.

TASTING NOTES

Sangria is, above all, a sociable drink. It is generally prepared in a jug so not designed for solitary drinking. This is a drink to enjoy with friends and family, ideally on a hot summer's day at a *chiringuito* (beachside bar) where you can sip your drink sitting on a stool with sand between your toes. Sangria should be drunk soon after it is made otherwise the ice will melt and it will go flat. At the same time, don't drink it too quickly! Remember that added liqueur – as innocuous and thirst-quenching as this delicious concoction tastes, it still has serious hangover potential! ● *by Josephine Quintero*

ORIGINS

Legend holds that the Chilean cocktail was invented shortly after the earthquake that rocked Valparaiso in 1985. It's said that the drink was first made on the request of a German journalist on a particularly hot summer day. After quickly drinking the concoction, he tried to stand up. He felt dizzy – and compared the effect to experiencing an earthquake.

SERVES 1

CHILE

TERREMOTO

The aptly named *terremoto* (earthquake) is a sweetly
potent cocktail made with white wine, a dash of liquor, and
– wait for it – pineapple ice cream, served in a large glass.

YOU'LL NEED

3–5 tablespoons pineapple
ice cream
240ml (8oz) white wine, to
taste
Fernet or grenadine, to taste

METHOD

1 In a large glass, add a scoop of pineapple ice cream.

2 Add the wine.

3 Top up the glass with the Fernet or grenadine. Add a straw
and serve immediately.

TASTING NOTES

Though the *terremoto* is considered a traditional Chilean cocktail, it's not
something you'll regularly find on a menu. It's a speciality to seek out at a classic
Santiago bar like La Piojera – one of the bars that claims to have invented it – where the
waiters carry large trays laden with glasses and the wooden tabletops quickly get sticky with
splashes of the creamy concoction. Typically, the *terremoto* is served with a straw. On the
first sip, it's like drinking a fruity milkshake – then you taste the acidity of the *pipeño*, a sweet
white wine, and the bitterness of the liquor. The first one goes down easy. Finish a second
one and the ground might start to feel unsteady.

The preparation of the *terremoto* varies slightly, depending on where it's served: at La
Piojera, the barmen use Fernet, while at El Hoyo, grenadine is the norm. Other traditional
bars use rum or cognac. ● *by Bridget Gleeson*

TASTING
NOTES
The World's Best Drinks

GIN

Throughout the ages, gin has been associated with every scene from the seedy slums of Georgian London to the manicured lawns of colonial India. The main flavour of this spirit has always been juniper, but these days distilleries produce batches with an ever-increasing range of delectably fragrant botanicals.

The powerful scent of gin makes it the perfect backbone for creative floral and citrus cocktails, and of course the classic Martini remains one of the most iconic cocktails ever mixed. As for the good old G&T, this is a drink that will never go out of style as long as there are pubs, barbecues, garden parties and long summer evenings. →

HISTORY

The earliest versions of gin were made by Dutch and Flemish distillers for medicinal purposes, but it was when the Brits got hold of the stuff that the spirit really came into its own. When the government allowed unlicensed production in the early 1700s, making gin cheap and easy to buy, England quite simply went berserk for it. London in particular entered a wild 50-year binge-drinking period known as the Gin Craze, which resulted in gin being blamed for everything from debauchery to crime and madness. It is said that Londoners each drank an average of 14 gallons of gin a year, until a series of Gin Acts finally reined in the trade and consumption dropped.

TASTING

The easiest, simplest way to drink gin is in a gin and tonic. Crisp and refreshing, it tastes best served long over plenty of ice, with a squeezed wedge of lime or lemon sitting on the edge of the glass. The basic brands of tonic water and gin that every pub stocks already make for a fine drink, but of course, there's nothing wrong with stepping things up a little. Pick your favourite gin then give it a lift with an artisanal tonic water. These small-batch tonics have come onto the market in recent years, using fresh, natural ingredients and avoiding high-fructose corn syrup as a sweetener. Alternatively, using a splash of tonic syrup to taste, mixed with soda water, is becoming a popular way to customise your G&T.

"ENGLAND QUITE SIMPLY WENT BERSERK FOR IT"

VARIANTS

There are three main styles of gin. London Dry is by far the most common variety – this'll be poured for you if you don't specify otherwise. The name doesn't necessarily mean it was distilled in London, but the production does have to keep to a set of rules – it can't have any artificial ingredients and it must be at least 70% ABV. The taste is clean, aromatic, and works beautifully with tonic or in a Martini.

Plymouth Gin is sweet, fruity and earthy. Historically, only gin made in Plymouth has been allowed to take the name and nowadays there's only one producer left that makes it. Two varieties are still available, the Original, and the Navy strength, which was popular with the British Navy in the late 18th century. Yes, the latter will knock your socks off.

Old Tom, also with London origins, is the sweetest and most syrupy of the styles. It's only recently become widely available. Unsurprisingly, it's the main ingredient in a Tom Collins cocktail.

Within these varieties, modern distillers have begun producing gins with such a wide variety of infusions they almost taste like different spirits – ask the bartender for herbal, floral, spicy or citrus-flavoured recommendations. ● *by Helen Elfer*

DID YOU KNOW?

Copious amounts of gin and tonic were drunk by the British army in the early 19th century because they believed the quinine in the tonic water would help ward off malaria. They added their gin rations, sugar and lime to improve the bitter taste.

ORIGINS

The origin of the Martini is as hotly disputed as how it should be mixed. Some say it evolved in the late 1880s when customers would order a Martinez in a San Francisco hotel before taking the ferry to the town of the same name. A more likely story is that the Martini is called after the Italian vermouth brand. Back then a 'gin and Martini' mixed in equal parts was a popular tipple, and over time the proportions changed but the name stuck.

SERVES 1

USA

MARTINI

Clear, cold and bitingly strong, the Martini is a drinker's drink and connoisseurs obsess over the details. Gin or vodka? Shaken or stirred? Wet, dry or dirty? And no, the Appletini is absolutely not one of the options.

YOU'LL NEED

ice cubes
50ml (1¾fl oz) gin
5ml (¼fl oz) vermouth
lemon peel or olives,
   to garnish

METHOD

1 Fill a cocktail shaker with ice cubes.

2 Slowly pour the gin and the vermouth over the ice and let it sit gently until the outside of the shaker is frosted.

3 Strain the liquid into a Martini glass.

4 Garnish with a twist of lemon peel, or three olives skewered on a cocktail stick.

TASTING NOTES

The drama of this drink begins as you soon as you ask for it – ideally while dressed to the nines in a glamorous bar. Other cocktail orders simply get a nod, but the Martini drinker is fired a round of questions about their precise specifications. Officially it's down to personal taste, but anyone who truly loves this drink always orders it with gin, bone dry and stirred. Martinis should never be shaken, as this dilutes the liquid and leaves it cloudy – sorry 007. Mr Bond was also partial to the vodka variety, but purists say a true Martini is made with gin.

There's almost as much to smell in a great gin Martini as in a complex wine – herbal, floral and spicy notes all waft from the glass as it's raised slowly to the lips. That first sip delivers an icy burn that slides from the mouth to the belly, and after that? Well, it's just intoxicating on every level. ● *by Helen Elfer*

ORIGINS

Sometimes a long drink simply doesn't hit the spot. Legend has it that Florentine count Camillo Negroni was in need of a beverage with more kick than his regular Americano. His mixologist dutifully fortified the Campari-vermouth blend with gin (rather than topping it with soda water). A classic Italian aperitivo was born.

SERVES 1

ITALY

NEGRONI

A good negroni invigorates, rather than intoxicates. With a fresh citrus scent and complex herbal notes, this Italian aperitivo is a superb palate-cleanser on a summer's evening.

YOU'LL NEED
3–4 ice cubes
35ml (1¼fl oz) gin
35ml (1¼fl oz) vermouth
35ml (1¼fl oz) Campari
1 slice of orange

METHOD
1 Tip the ice cubes into a short whisky glass and pour on the gin, vermouth and Campari.

2 Stir quickly with a cocktail spoon before topping with the orange slice. *Salute!*

TASTING NOTES
On warm Italian evenings, there's no rush to reach the dinner table. As the sun begins to dip, hours are spent lingering over buttery Castelvetrano olives or bruschetta crowned with tomato and basil. And always accompanied by an aperitivo like the negroni.

The clink of ice as it swirls in a glass of negroni has an almost Pavlovian effect. Aperitivi are intended to whet the appetite, but they are also woven into social ritual. As with other aperitivi, this ruby nectar holds the promise of languorous hours spent sipping and socialising before a meal.

This simple three-spirit blend produces wonderfully complex flavours. The bright grapefruit scent is balanced by bitter herbal notes. The garnish, a freshly cut orange wedge, adds a sweet, tangy fragrance. ● *by Anita Isalska*

ORIGINS

Mr James Pimm sold his London oyster-bar clients a 'digestive tonic' in the 19th century: a secret mix of spirits, quinine and spices. Served in a tankard known as a 'No 1 cup', the drink (and brand) was sold in 1865, and while it has changed hands several times and diversified, offering cup numbers 2 to 7, today it is owned by the Diageo conglomerate, and only numbers 1, 6 and a 'Winter Cup' remain.

MAKES A PITCHER FOR 4

UNITED KINGDOM

PIMM'S

The quintessential taste of British summer, a jug of this gin-based, tea-coloured, citrus drink tropically topped with fruit and mint is mandatory at picnics and sporting events across the nation.

YOU'LL NEED

250ml (8fl oz) Pimm's no 1
½ cucumber, chopped
1 orange, sliced
squeeze of lemon juice
handful of mint, crushed
  gently
1l (24fl oz) lemonade (best
  quality you can find)
3 strawberries, sliced
ice

METHOD

1 Mix the Pimm's, cucumber, orange, lemon and mint together and refrigerate for an hour to let the flavours intensify.

2 Pour the Pimm's concoction into a jug half-filled with ice.

3 Add the lemonade, then the strawberries just before serving, so they're not too soggy.

4 Stir everything together gently. Party time.

TASTING NOTES

I say, it's Pimm's o'clock. Anyone for Pimm's? Can you hear the thwack of tennis balls? Of cricket ball on bat? Of horses hooves thundering down a polo pitch? Find a grassy spot, shake out your picnic rug and submit to the Jug Pourer, while shielding your eyes from the sun. You'll likely get a good hunk of ice, a wodge of strawberry or orange, and some layers of cucumber and mint, along with the fizzy tawny mixture that tumbles into your glass and splashes your hand. Guzzle eagerly for the refreshing, slightly spicy overtones and nibble the juicy, gin-macerated fruit. Applaud the shot, the catch, the goal. Nudge the Jug Pourer again. Or even smarter, appoint yourself Jug Pourer next time. ● *by Karyn Noble*

ORIGINS

Widely regarded as Singapore's national drink, the Sling was created in 1915 at Raffles Singapore's famous Long Bar. As the story (or at least one of them) goes, bartender Ngiam Tong Boon created it so ladies could sneakily enjoy a gin (disguised as fruit punch) alongside the gentlemen at a time when etiquette dictated women couldn't drink alcohol in public. It's thought the original recipe was lost during the 1930s, and it has been hotly contested ever since.

SERVES 1

SINGAPORE

SINGAPORE SLING

Modern mixologists may have moved on from the traditional recipe, but for a real taste of colonial Singapore, it's impossible to beat this classic tiki bar tipple.

YOU'LL NEED
30ml (1fl oz) dry gin
15ml (0½fl oz) Cherry Heering
  liqueur, cherry brandy or
  kirsch
8ml (⅓fl oz) Bénédictine
8ml (⅓fl oz) Cointreau
75ml (2½fl oz) pineapple juice
15ml (½fl oz) lime juice
8ml (⅓fl oz) grenadine
1 dash Angostura bitters
soda water
pineapple slice and
  maraschino cherry
  to garnish
ice

METHOD
1 Add all the ingredients, except the soda and garnishes, to a cocktail shaker half-filled with ice.

2 Shake and strain into a tall, ice-filled glass.

3 Top with soda, lightly stir and garnish with the pineapple slice and cherry.

TASTING NOTES
The perfect pick-me-up on a sultry equatorial afternoon – for the Sling was specifically designed to be imbibed in its birthplace – the exotic ingredients in this sparkling scarlet concoction combine to deliver a sharp, fruity slap of sweetness with a seductive herbal undertone. These days many deem the original recipe too sweet, the cherry flavour too dominating. But when served fresh in the right climate, not to mention the right bar (Raffles Singapore's Long Bar looks much as it did a century ago, complete with rattan-fan 'air-con'), this colonial-era quencher still hits the spot. ● *by Sarah Reid*

ORIGINS

Sloe gin has a slightly shameful
past. The berry-like fruit grows
from blackthorn bushes, which
are riddled with savage thorns:
    ideal security fences for the
ruling elite in 18th century Britain, when thousands of people
were kicked off common land.
Too bitter to eat, sloes were
soaked in two commodities that
were cheap at the time: gin (the
Government allowed unlicensed
    gin production) and sugar (a
result of the slave trade in the
West Indies). Sloe gin enjoys a
respectable renaissance these
days, however – just ask your
       hipster mixologist.

UNITED KINGDOM

SLOE GIN

The first surprise? Technically, it's not a gin. The second? Making sloe gin is slow. But this ruby-red liqueur of sloe fruits soaked in sugar and gin rewards those who wait.

MAKES 1 LITRE

YOU'LL NEED

500g (1lb) sloes (preferably handpicked when ripe and softened by the first frost, although don't wait for this if the berries are already ripe – a frost may not happen!)
250g (8oz) sugar
1l (34fl oz) gin
4 drops vanilla essence (optional)

METHOD

1 Wash the sloes and prick each one with a pin (seven times, if you like to follow tradition). Leave them to air-dry.

2 When dry, put the sloes in a sealable jar and pour over the sugar, gin, and add the vanilla essence. Seal the jar and shake.

3 Shake the jar a little every other day for the first week, until the sugar dissolves. Then shake the jar once a week for two months.

4 You can sample your sloe gin after two months has passed, but it's best to leave it for at least three months. For a truly outstanding sloe gin, leave to macerate for 15 years, if you can wait that long!

5 When you're ready, or can't wait any longer, strain the gin into screw-top bottles.

6 Serve it neat, over ice, and/or with a little tonic water.

TASTING NOTES

Picking sloes yourself is half the fun (thorns aside) but don't be tempted to try a sloe straight from the bush! Tongue-shrivelling in tannic dryness, it's not a pleasant experience. Far better to gather your purple bounty in a wicker foraging basket and stumble home through the early autumn leaves to crack open last year's batch of gleaming-red sloe gin. Pour over ice with a little tonic water and kick off your sodden shoes, battleworn by hedgerow stomping, to settle by an open fire for your first sip. Sniff the slightly plummy, almond-like aroma and swirl the smooth sweetness in your mouth. The tartness follows, but it's not too sharp – only dry enough to hasten the next rich, warming sip. ● by Karyn Noble

ORIGINS

Most historians agree Tom is a descendant of a fizzy Jenever (from Holland) gin and lemon cocktail originated by one John Collins at Limmer's hotel in London and popular in the mid-1800s. Imbibed on American shores, theories abound concerning the name change: a nod to the use of Old Tom Gin? Or capitalising on a famous 1874 hoax that saw punters running from bar to bar in New York, in search of the fictitious scallywag 'Tom Collins' who was supposedly talking about them?

SERVES 1

USA

TOM COLLINS

A beloved summer classic combining gin, lemon, sugar and soda, this American cooler evolved from English roots and solidified its independence with a name change and its own special tumbler.

YOU'LL NEED

ice cubes
60ml (2fl oz) Old Tom or
  London dry gin
30ml (1fl oz) simple syrup (see
  below)
30ml (1fl oz) freshly squeezed
  lemon juice
soda water
slice of lemon, lime or
  grapefruit
maraschino cherry

METHOD

1 Fill a Tom Collins glass ¾ full with ice cubes.

2 Add gin, simple syrup (see below) and lemon to the glass.

3 Add soda water to fill the glass close to the rim.

4 Stir to ensure components are mixed.

5 Add a citrus slice and a maraschino cherry to garnish.

TIP *To prepare a simple syrup, combine equal volumes of water and sugar in a small saucepan. Heat over a medium heat, and stir until sugar dissolves. Cool. This will keep refrigerated for at least a month.*

TASTING NOTES

Few cocktails herald summer's arrival better than Tom Collins, and he's always ready to oblige when you're in need of a refined thirst quencher. Imbibing is all too easy: each sip delivering a burst of sun-splashed citrus through the effervescence, while the gin gives you a potent kick on its way down. Tom's waiting for you and your friends anywhere along the Eastern seaboard on a lazy, hazy afternoon, and he's also long associated with sportsmen, fitting nicely in hand for social spectator events such as tennis or horse racing. Should you win your bets, consider swapping the soda for champagne for a more sophisticated and celebratory 'French 75'. ● *by Caroline Veldhuis*

TASTING NOTES
The World's Best Drinks

VODKA

As Russian as Red Square, as Ukrainian as Yulia Tymoshenko and as Polish as Pope Jean-Paul II, vodka is the firewater of choice for some 300 million people, spread out in a 3000 mile sweep across the former Communist bloc. From Warsaw to Vladivostok, drinkers wax lyrical about the potency of this legendary colourless spirit, prepared using everything from rye and wheat to potatoes and sugar beet molasses. In the rest of the world, vodka is seen as the perfect mixer, with its neutral taste and powerful alcohol kick. Native drinkers prefer it neat, served in shot glass after shot glass after shot glass; it's no coincidence that the word 'vodka' is a corruption of the Russian word for water! →

HISTORY

Poland and Russia both claim to have invented vodka around the 9th century, but the first official record appears in the Vyatka Chronicle, written in Russia in 1174. Early vodkas were murky brews, full of impurities and capable of producing epic hangovers, despite attempts to clarify the fluid using isinglass, a natural gelatin removed from the swim bladders of sturgeon. Mass consumption of vodka didn't really take off until the 15th century, with the invention of pot distillation, and the creation of vodkas that didn't leave drinkers feeling like they had been trampled underfoot by the entire Russian Army.

TASTING

It's cold outside. You can tell because there's frost on the inside of the windows. A border guard barks a command in Russian and an orderly appears with a bottle of Русский Стандарт (Russian Standard) and two shot glasses... Even if you can't recreate the full Cold War ambiance at home, the essential first step is to chill your vodka to the right temperature – aim for around -18°C – and serve in a chilled shot glass. That way, the subtle tones that follow the initial blast of fire won't be swamped by the alcohol. Look for hints of other flavours – a sweetness, a smidgeon of buttery creaminess or a citrusy tang – all marks of a superior vodka. Sip, don't swig, then chase with a bite of pickle or preserved herring. Only a philistine would drink vodka without food!

VARIANTS

The great thing about vodka is that it can be made from almost anything. Wheat, rye, sorghum, potatoes, sugar beet, grapes, soya beans, sugar, even milk whey and wood fibres. Almost anything that ferments can be distilled down to produce precious drops of ethanol. However, in the modern age, the vast majority of vodkas are made from grains, with wheat and rye marking out the premium brands. Differences between premium vodkas are subtle – a lemony tang here, a slight sweetness there. Comparing good vodka to bad vodka is like comparing Napoléon cognac to kerosene. Flavoured vodkas are the latest darling of the drinks industry, though not of true vodka aficionados. You'll find vodkas spruced up with everything from raspberries and mango to cinnamon and salty liquorice. ● *by Joe Bindloss*

DID YOU KNOW?

Vodka was originally invented as a medicine. In the medieval period, this fearsome firewater was used as a tincture for treating everything from depression to the common cold. It even found a role in the production of gunpowder, used to dampen the powder grains during grinding to prevent spontaneous explosions!

ORIGINS

The Bloody Mary was born in 1920s Paris at Harry's New York Bar. Barman Fernand Petiot combined Russian vodka (distilled in Paris by immigrants who had fled the Russian Revolution) with canned tomato juice, newly imported from America. The drink was christened by one of its first samplers, American musician Roy Barton, after the Chicago nightclub Bucket of Blood and its waitress, Mary.

SERVES 1

PARIS, FRANCE

BLOODY MARY

With its feisty vodka kick, zing of lemon and spicy Tabasco, the Bloody Mary is guaranteed to give your senses a wake-up call: its reputation as a hangover cure is legendary.

YOU'LL NEED

60ml (2fl oz) vodka
120ml (4fl oz) tomato juice
1 tbs freshly squeezed lemon
   juice
pinch of salt
pinch of finely ground black
   pepper
1 tsp Tabasco sauce (or a
   pinch of finely ground
   cayenne pepper)
3 tsp Worcestershire sauce
1 large ice cube
1 celery stick, to garnish
1 lemon wedge, to garnish

METHOD

1 Place all of the ingredients except the garnishes in a cocktail shaker or a tightly sealed screw-top jar. Shake vigorously for 10–15 seconds.

2 Strain into a 240ml (8fl oz) highball glass.

3 Garnish with the celery stick and lemon wedge.

4 Enjoy!

TASTING NOTES

Sharp, piquant, and refreshingly savoury, a Bloody Mary is ideal at any time of year, with the spicy heat balanced by the cooling tomato juice. It is often described as 'the world's most complex cocktail' and crimes witnessed in bars around the world include the quantity of Worcestershire sauce outweighing the amount of tomato juice in the glass, and the unforgivable sin of substituting tomato juice for dry, powdered tomato soup mix. Much more successful variations involve swapping vodka for gin, adding horseradish, or garnishing with olives. ● *by Catherine Le Nevez*

MATT MUNRO © LONELY PLANET IMAGES, STEVE BROWN PHOTOGRAPHY © GETTY IMAGES

ORIGINS

The Caesar owes its invention to Walter Chell, a restaurant manager who set out in 1969 to create a signature cocktail for the Calgary Inn's new Italian eatery. Using Italy's spaghetti *alle vongole* as his inspiration, he experimented with tomato juice, clam nectar, vodka, Worcestershire sauce and other spices until the Caesar was born. Its popularity soon spread across the nation, and it's now the most consumed mixed drink in Canada – some 350 million are savoured each year.

SERVES 1

CANADA

CAESAR

Some drinks gently kiss your palate, others slap you in the face.
The Caesar, with its sweet, savoury and bitter flavours, is definitely
not of the kissing variety. But you'll love it just the same.

YOU'LL NEED

1 lime wedge
celery salt
ice
30ml (1fl oz) vodka
120–180ml (4–6fl oz) Mott's
    Clamato juice
2 dashes of hot sauce (such
    as Tabasco)
3 dashes salt
3 dashes freshly ground
    pepper
4 dashes of Worcestershire
    sauce
1 celery stick

METHOD

1 Run a wedge of lime around the top of the highball glass
before dipping the rim into celery salt. Set the lime wedge
aside.

2 Add the ice, vodka and Clamato juice before seasoning with
Tabasco, salt, pepper and Worcestershire sauce.

3 Garnish with a celery stick and the wedge of lime.

TASTING NOTES

Fortune favours the brave, and the Caesar is no exception. Those who get over
the psychological 'clam barrier' and indulge in this powerful lip-smacking mixed
cocktail will never look back. You'll see their satisfied faces on many a Canadian bar patio
– just listen for the crunch of celery. The Caesar's rich red colour and ornate garnishes,
which can also include gherkins or pickled beans, ensure it always makes a grand entrance
to any social situation (in Canada its arrival is typically greeted by knowing nods from other
patrons). Once in hand, the heady mix of ingredients, which can be tailored to your love of
spice, will not only rock your taste buds, but also your sense of smell. ● by Matt Phillips

ORIGINS

The state of Massachusetts is the second largest producer of cranberries in the US, so perhaps it's not surprising that the Cape Codder's key ingredients are vodka and cranberry juice. The drink's origins are murkier than a cranberry bog, though. While it became popular with New England's preppy set after the Ocean Spray Cranberry Cooperative introduced its Cranberry Juice Cocktail in the 1930s, California's Trader Vic's Restaurant also claims to have created this bracing cranberry drink.

USA

CAPE CODDER

Named after the beach-lined Cape Cod peninsula in the Eastern United States, this refreshingly tart cranberry beverage is a traditional happy-hour cocktail that transports you to summertime at the shore.

YOU'LL NEED
60ml (2fl oz) vodka
120–150ml (4–5fl oz)
  cranberry juice
½ lime, plus a lime wedge to
  garnish

METHOD
1 Fill a tall cocktail glass with ice and pour in the vodka.

2 Add the cranberry juice.

3 Squeeze the lime, and add lime juice to taste. Stir.

4 Garnish drink with a lime wedge, and serve.

TASTING NOTES
The best place to sip a Cape Codder is on Cape Cod, of course. Picture a summer evening on a patio overlooking the ocean, with a salty breeze blowing. A lazy afternoon with your feet in the sand. Or cocktail hour at a beachfront seafood shack, where a lobster roll or a bucket of steamers (clams) await. But wherever you are, you can enjoy this simple, almost old-fashioned cocktail. The tart fruit refresher doesn't call for any exotic ingredients or complicated infusions. Just make some ice cubes and set out your tall glasses. Then pull on a polo shirt and Bermuda shorts, or a filmy summer dress, and you're ready to relish this classic, happy-hour beverage.

While many Cape Cod purists insist on adding lime, you can substitute lemon. Add club soda if you prefer a lighter, sparkling drink. ● *by Carolyn Heller*

© TIM E WHITE

ORIGINS

'The Cosmo' as it's affection-
ately known, started life in small
drinking subcultures in the US,
though its official creator is
hotly disputed. It became the
'It' cocktail for a generation of
women and gay men in the late
1990s, peaking as the frequently
referenced drink of choice for
Carrie, Miranda, Samantha and
Charlotte before fizzing fickley
out of favour to become a
standard on the classics menu.
That's fashion for you.

SERVES 1

USA

COSMOPOLITAN

Synonymous with style, sophistication and TV's *Sex and the City*, this pink concoction of cranberry juice, lime, Cointreau and vodka served in a martini glass is recognisable to fashionistas at fifty paces.

YOU'LL NEED

30ml (1fl oz) vodka (the best you can get – citrus-flavoured vodka also works well)

15ml (½fl oz) Cointreau (can be substituted with Triple Sec)

25ml (¾fl oz) cranberry juice (use more or less for personal preference and aesthetics; in addition to flavour, the amount of cranberry defines the cocktail's pink hue)

squeeze of fresh lime juice

ice

twist of orange peel, to serve

METHOD

1 Put a martini glass in the freezer to chill.

2 Put all the ingredients (apart from the orange peel) in a cocktail shaker, fill with ice and shake hard for about 20 seconds.

3 Strain into your chilled martini glass.

4 Peel a loop of orange zest over the top of the drink, hopefully catching a little orange oil in the glass as you do so.

5 For a bit more flamboyance, hold the orange peel with your thumb and forefinger and flame gently with a match for about 20 seconds, then add the burnt peel to garnish.

6 Enjoy, in fabulous fashion.

TASTING NOTES

For the authentic Cosmopolitan experience, get yourself to New York City, baby, and do your best *Sex and the City* impersonation. Slip on designer heels, an eye-catching outfit, and accessorise with your best bling. This is all about working it. Grab a couple of girlfriends, gay friends or a hot date and slink into a happening bar. 'Cosmo, please' you purr at the bartender, who's heard it all before. As the round of pretty pink drinks arrive, take your chilled martini glass and toast your fabulous posse/potential paramour. The first sweet sip – the refreshing cranberry and lime juice – initially masks the alcoholic effects of the vodka and Cointreau. But after a few, almost anyone may be looking fabulous. Keep your dignity, you sexy thing. ● *by Karyn Noble*

ORIGINS

This decadent use of espresso and its chic presentation hint at Italian flair. But the Espresso Martini originates deep in the smoulder and sleaze of 1980s London. It was first shaken up in Soho bar Fred's, after a glamorous patron asked for a drink to wake her up and then knock her out. The lady's name – and the rather more colourful phrasing of her request – are lost. But the drink endured to ignite the taste buds (and energy levels) of cocktail lovers worldwide.

SERVES 1

LONDON, UNITED KINGDOM

ESPRESSO MARTINI

An Espresso Martini is the tuxedo of the cocktail world. Sophisticated, rich and midnight-dark, this sultry drink blends quality espresso, vodka and Kahlúa in a Martini glass.

YOU'LL NEED

40ml (1½fl oz) espresso
1 cup ice cubes, straight from the freezer
25ml (¾fl oz) Kahlúa (or other coffee liqueur)
35ml (1¼fl oz) vodka
5ml (¼fl oz) sugar syrup (optional)
2-3 whole roasted coffee beans

METHOD

1 Use a quality espresso machine to brew a strong shot of espresso.

2 Fill a cocktail shaker with ice cubes before pouring 40ml of espresso, the Kahlúa, vodka and sugar syrup over it.

3 Shake heartily for about 20 seconds.

4 Open the shaker and use a cocktail sieve (or the lid) to strain the liquid into a Martini glass, excluding the ice cubes.

5 A supple foam should have formed on the drink. Float the coffee beans in the centre and serve.

TASTING NOTES

A beautifully blended Espresso Martini seduces you first with its scent: a whisper of caramel and chocolate, before the rich odour of coffee barrels into your nostrils. From the first sip, your taste buds should flood with coffee flavours, a dash of sweetness from the Kahlúa balancing any bitter notes. Respect the Espresso Martini like a vengeful coffee god: the collision of caffeine rush and mellowing vodka can wield a wicked power.

Scout an espresso machine before you order, to avoid inferior imitations made with the dreaded instant coffee. The best adaptations are found in coffee cultures like Melbourne and NYC. ● *by Anita Isalska*

ORIGINS

We suspect that Thailand was secretly fuming that the Mai Tai came from California and that Singapore had its famous sling. The time was ripe for a uniquely Thai cocktail, and in 2009, the Siam Sunray was born. Concocted by award-winning bartender Surasakdi Pantaisong as part of a tourist board campaign, this unlikely sounding drink blends the elements of *tom yam* with syrup, vodka and lime – it probably shouldn't work, but somehow, in the sweltering heat of a Bangkok evening, it tastes just right.

SERVES 1

BANGKOK, THAILAND

SIAM SUNRAY

A generous serving of Asian cooking spices transforms the Siam Sunray from vodka cocktail to 'Thailand in a glass' – sit back on a Thai beach and imbibe!

YOU'LL NEED

½ Thai chilli pepper
3 thin slices of ginger
1 Kaffir lime leaf
3 thin slivers of lemongrass
15ml (½fl oz) sugar syrup
3 drops lime juice
40ml (1½fl oz) vodka
30ml (1fl oz) coconut liqueur
  (or coconut-flavoured
  Bacardi – avoid Malibu)
ice
a splash of soda water
chilli pepper, to garnish
lime wedge, to garnish

METHOD

1 Crush the chilli, ginger, lime leaf and lemongrass together in a shaker to bring out the flavours, and rouse the aroma.

2 Add the syrup, lime juice, vodka and coconut liqueur and do your best Tom Cruise impression.

3 Once shaken, strain into a long glass over ice, top up with soda water, and garnish with a fresh chilli pepper and lime. Bingo, *tom yam* in a glass!

TASTING NOTES

For now, the Siam Sunray is nowhere near as ubiquitous as the Singapore Sling, but it's a slow burner, appearing in more and more bars and restaurants around the Kingdom of Smiles. The fresh chilli resting on the rim of the glass should give you the first indication of the flavours waiting inside. The initial sip delivers a powerful tang of lemongrass and lime, helped by a double dose of lime juice and kaffir lime leaves. Then there's the smoothness of syrup and coconut, which soon gives way to the alcoholic scorch of vodka and the tickle of ginger and hot chilli. We can't promise you'll want to keep drinking it all night, but it's definitely more thrilling than another bottle of Chang. Luckily, there's an official recipe for the Siam Sunray, so it's easy to make at home! ● *by Joe Bindloss*

© DANIEL DI PAOLO

TASTING NOTES
The World's Best Drinks

RUM

There is considerable debate about where the word 'rum' comes from – some say it's the name of a Dutch drinking glass, others claim it comes from *saccharum*, the Roman word for sugar – but perhaps the most compelling explanation is that the popular name for this distilled, fermented sugar cane spirit comes from the slang word rumbullion, meaning 'uproar'. This flavoursome and eminently mixable spirit certainly took the nautical world by storm, becoming the favoured quaff of slaves, spice-traders, sailors and pirates, and later of cocktail-makers trying to conjure up the romance of the seafaring life in a glass. Sipped neat or on the rocks, or used as the foundation stone for myriad cocktails, rum is arguably the world's favourite spirit, and certainly its most versatile. →

HISTORY

Ask anyone where rum was invented and almost everyone would pick a palm-fringed island in the Caribbean. So it might come as a surprise to learn that, as with most things, the Chinese were fermenting sugar cane juice around a thousand years before Europeans stumbled across the Americas. But credit where credit is due – it was the plantation owners of the Caribbean, and more importantly their slaves, who worked out that fermented cane juice could be distilled into the finest firewater this side of Port Royal. By the 16th century, every pirate and seafarer worth his salt had a taste for the drink known as 'kill-devil' – and the rest is history.

TASTING

Before taking that fiery first sip, every rum-drinker should nail their colours to the mast. Are you a white rum drinker, more concerned with the medley of rum tones and mixers, or are you a card-carrying aficionado of spiced rums that swim with the flavour of the Caribbean, or dark rum aged on pirate ships in old oak barrels? Whatever your poison, rum tastes like what it was made from – caramel, sugar, molasses – transported on a smooth alcohol base that is perfect for sipping or mixing. To fully appreciate a dark rum, sip it neat at room temperature; after the initial fire, look for subtle overtones of vanilla, Caribbean spices, combustion and smoke.

"EVERY PIRATE WORTH HIS SALT HAD A TASTE FOR THE DRINK"

DID YOU KNOW?

According to popular legend, Admiral Lord Nelson's body was preserved in a barrel of rum after the Battle of Trafalgar. As the story goes, thirsty sailors tapped into the barrel and drained the contents, earning rum the nickname 'Nelson's Blood'. However, some historians refute the story, claiming it was actually brandy!

VARIANTS

There are almost as many varieties of rum as there are nations that grow sugar cane. The drink that most people think of as rum is conventionally made from fermented molasses, often spiced for added punch, but unrefined sugar cane juice is used as a base for the *rhum* produced on French-speaking Caribbean islands such as Martinique, Guadeloupe and Haiti.

Sugar cane juice is also the base for dozens of hooch-like aguardiente spirits produced across Latin America, and for Brazilian cachaça, which gains extra flavour from added cane sugar and maturation in aged barrels. Africa gets in on the action too, with sugar cane spirits such as 'CJ' ('cane juice', obviously), the favoured firewater in Liberia.

Adding flavouring to rum is as old as the spice trade. Classic spiced rums come with heady overtones of brown sugar, vanilla, cinnamon, allspice, cloves and pepper, conjuring up images of pirate brigantines roaming the Caribbean. Then there are the flavoured rums that no purist would touch outside of a cocktail glass – sticky coconut Malibu and super sweet coffee-flavoured Kahlua and Tia Maria. ● *by Joe Bindloss*

ORIGINS

Simply (that word again),
the daiquiri was born out of
necessity – the gin ran out,
and local ingredients – lime,
sugar and rum – saved the
day! Thank the stars for that.
Commonly attributed to a US
mining guy based in Cuba in the
late 19th century (who obviously
misjudged his gin stocks!) and
named after a beach nearby,
the drink became popular in the
early 1900s and then boomed
as it became the drink of choice
for Hemingway and F. Scott
Fitzgerald.

SERVES 1

CUBA

DAIQUIRI

Simplicity and perfection – there's no other way to describe a daiquiri. We're not talking frozen daiquiri abominations, we're talking three ingredients: rum, sugar and lime juice. A drink so much greater than the sum of its parts...

YOU'LL NEED

60ml (2fl oz) white rum
30ml (1fl oz) lime juice
15ml (½fl oz) sugar syrup
ice
slice of lime

METHOD

1 Put a martini glass or champagne coupe in the freezer to chill.

2 In a cocktail shaker, combine the three ingredients with a handful of ice.

3 Shake until it's icy cold.

4 Pour into your chilled glass.

5 Make a cut into your lime slice to the centre of the circle and hang it on the rim of the glass.

TASTING NOTES

The pleasure of a daiquiri begins with making it. The measuring of rum, sugar syrup (trust us) and lime juice, the shaker full of ice. Preparing a perfect slice of lime. Chilling a martini glass. It's all easy and you know you're building up to something great. Your mouth will water.

Once strained into the glass, what happens next depends: it's the beautiful thing about a daiquiri – you can sip it solo and let its freshness and zing become a meditation, or you can party with it on a beach in Cuba and let the rum get you jabbering enthusiastically. You might even pen a great work after a few of them. Regardless of the mode, this sweet, sour, strong and cold drink will fill your palate and make you happy. So very very happy. ● *by Ben Handicott*

ORIGINS

Sailors have always loved dark rum, and in the 1800s the British Royal Navy even included 2oz of the stuff as part of standard daily rations. So when the Royal Navy's dockyard on Ireland Island in Bermuda constructed a ginger beer plant around the turn of the 20th century, it was only a matter of time before the two ingredients ended up in a drink together. When they did, the Dark and Stormy was born.

SERVES 1

BERMUDA

DARK AND STORMY

A tempest in a teapot? Certainly not! The sweet flavours of this rum-based ginger cocktail need to be shouted about. Indulge in them, rain or shine.

YOU'LL NEED

120–150ml (4–5fl oz) ginger beer
40–60ml (1½–2fl oz) dark rum
ice
wedge of lime

METHOD

1 Pour the ginger beer into an ice-filled glass. Follow with dark rum.

2 Garnish your Dark and Stormy with a wedge of lime.

TASTING NOTES

It shouldn't come as any surprise that the Dark and Stormy is the national drink of Bermuda – it crushes thirst, puts smiles on faces and slows the pace of life to a pedestrian affair. Thankfully it has a similar effect wherever it is enjoyed, and whatever the weather (though Bermuda shorts are never mandatory).

How much bite your tipple has is up to you, with a wide range of sweetness and spice available in the various brands of ginger beer and dark rum. Just never, ever, make the mistake of trying to mix one with ginger ale, the anaemic distant cousin (thrice removed) of the beer variety. ● *by Matt Phillips*

ORIGINS

Eggnog is generally thought to be a descendant of the medieval English `posset`: a hot milk toddy laced with ale, then sweetened and spiced. But it was the American colonies that really took the bull by the horns in the 18th century, ditching the English booze in favour of free-flowing whiskey and later rum, and made eggnog the ubiquitous yuletide staple that Americans (more so than Brits) love today.

UNITED KINGDOM

EGGNOG

SERVES 2

Christmas wouldn't be Christmas without this custard-in-a-cup cocktail descended from an English medieval tipple. An unlikely marriage of raw eggs, milk and alcohol, a good batch of eggnog should be creamy, frothy and sweet.

YOU'LL NEED

2 large eggs
2tbsp caster sugar
100ml (3½fl oz) alcohol of your choice: sherry, Madeira or brandy if you're channelling the English; whiskey, rum or bourbon if you're after an American flavour
200ml (7fl oz) full-fat milk
150ml (5fl oz) double cream or whipping cream
grated nutmeg

METHOD

1 Separate your eggs into yolks and whites.

2 Whisk the egg yolks with the caster sugar until pale and fluffy. Save your arms and use an electric whisk for this step.

3 Add your chosen booze to the eggs-and-sugar mixture a little at a time, then the milk. Be warned that the mixture may separate if you leave it standing a while. If this happens, give it another whisk.

4 In a separate bowl, whisk the egg whites to the point where they form soft peaks and then fold this mixture into the boozy egg concoction.

5 In another bowl, whip the cream until it becomes slightly stiff and then fold this into the mixture too.

6 Pour the eggnog straight into glasses and dust with nutmeg before serving, or refrigerate the mixture for up to 24 hours. (As it contains raw egg, it's not advisable to keep it any longer).

TASTING NOTES

Eggnog is the Marmite of the festive drinks cabinet: you either love it or hate it, and there's nothing quite like it to split the Christmas party down the middle. Whipped up right, it should be rich and creamy but still light and frothy; sweet but not sickly, and always with a great wallop of heat at the end from generous ladles of booze. Such are its dessert-like qualities that it's a rare thing to see a merry soul manage to knock back more than one or two glasses. Aspiring mixologists beware: when it goes wrong, it goes very wrong (lumpy custard, anyone?). ● *by Lorna Parkes*

ORIGINS

Rich in antioxidants and vitamin C, the petals of the Jamaican sorrel have been used to make a refreshing herbal infusion in West Africa (where it originates), Latin America (where it is called *agua de Jamaica*) and the Caribbean for centuries. As the pink flowers generally reach maturity in December, it's little surprise that this beverage has been adopted as Jamaica's favourite Christmas drink.

MAKES 1 LARGE JUG

JAMAICA

HIBISCUS GINGER PUNCH

If the Caribbean came in a cup, it'd taste something like this deep-rouge tropical summer cooler, made from hibiscus flowers and toughened up with a liberal splash of rum.

YOU'LL NEED

500g (16 oz) dried Jamaican hibiscus (sorrel) flowers
60ml (2 oz) minced fresh ginger
2l (3½ pints) boiling water
150g agave syrup (or substitute for 8 oz raw sugar)
amber rum to taste (use Appleton Estate for Jamaican authenticity)
2 fresh lemons or limes, cut into wedges
2 cups ice cubes
mint, to garnish

METHOD

1 Place the hibiscus flowers and ginger in a large heatproof bowl. Pour in the boiling water.

2 Cover the bowl and allow the mixture to steep for 1–2 hours.

3 Stir in the agave or sugar.

4 Strain the mixture into a large pitcher.

5 Chill the drink in the fridge.

6 Once the drink is cold and you are ready to serve it, add lightly squeezed lemon or lime wedges to the pitcher, along with rum to taste, and the ice.

7 Stir to combine everything. Garnish with a sprig of mint and serve.

TASTING NOTES

There aren't many other blooms that scream summer quite like pink hibiscus. And its flowers really are good enough to eat – when infused in water, it produces a deliciously tart crimson cordial similar to cranberry juice. It is commonly served as an agua fresca (fresh water) by street vendors and bodegas across Mexico and Central America. It's also a popular tea. But the addition of sugar (which balances out the hibiscus), ginger (for extra zing), and a splash of rum (it's Jamaican, after all) takes it to the next level. Sweet, tangy and deliciously exotic, it's the ultimate sweaty-day quencher. All that's missing is a plate of jerk chicken – or a cheeky slice of Jamaican fruitcake. ● *by Sarah Reid*

ORIGINS

In 1944, Vic 'The Trader'
Bergaron mixed a drink for his
Tahitian friends at his legendary
Bay Area bar, Trader Vic's.
'Maita'i roa ae!' they exclaimed
when they tasted it (which means
'very good!' in Tahitian), and
thus, the quintessential tiki drink
and unofficial cocktail of the
South Pacific was born. In time,
bartenders added ingredients
like pineapple or passion fruit
juices and switched the orange
curacao for triple sec; the drink
continues to evolve.

SERVES 1

CALIFORNIA & POLYNESIA

MAI TAI

Fruity and rum-heavy, a mai tai is like a vacation in a glass. Jetsetters sip them in Bora Bora, but anyone can enjoy one and dream of the tropics.

YOU'LL NEED

1 cup crushed ice
60ml (2fl oz) rum (preferably 17-year-old J. Wray Nephew or Denizen's Merchant Reserve)
15ml (½fl oz) French orgeat syrup
15ml (½fl oz) orange curacao
8ml (⅓fl oz) rock candy or simple syrup
juice of one lime
1 cup ice cubes
1 sprig fresh mint
fruit garnish, optional

METHOD

1 Fill a highball glass with the crushed ice and place in the freezer.

2 Combine all liquid ingredients with the cup of ice cubes in a cocktail shaker and shake until chilled.

3 Remove the highball glass from the freezer.

4 Strain the cocktail from the ice cubes into the highball glass and crushed ice.

5 Garnish with the mint sprig and optional fruit.

6 Serve with a straw.

TASTING NOTES

Sipping a mai tai is as close as you can get to drinking a South Seas sunset. Hints of flower-scented air come from the sweetness of the syrups; the tartness of ocean spray is added via lime juice; a splash of tropical colour is blended in with the orange curacao; and a warm sense of tranquility flows with the boozy aged rum. If you can't dip your feet in sparkling sands and blue waters, the next best thing is to enjoy a mai tai – or try one at a Tiki bar for a fun and authentic taste of mid-century kitsch. ● *by Celeste Brash*

ORIGINS

The mojito's roots sink deep into the Cuban countryside, which makes sense, given the ingredients: limes prevented scurvy among colonial sailors and sugar cane fields blanket the hinterlands. No one knows who first brought these elements together to create the mojito. But the drink's ascendancy can be traced, first, to 1930s Havana, and then to the cocktail culture of the early 21st century.

SERVES 1

MOJITO

Sultry and refreshing, a mojito is the rare island drink that is both sugary and herbaceous, an organic experience that takes the edge off a humid, tropical day wonderfully.

YOU'LL NEED

1 tsp sugar
1 lime, cut into wedges
1 sprig mint
4 oz crushed ice
60–120ml (2–4fl oz) white rum
240ml (8fl oz) club soda

METHOD

1 Put the sugar into a 12-ounce glass.

2 Squeeze around 30-60ml of juice from the lime into the glass, then add a lime wedge.

3 Place the sprig of mint into the glass.

4 Use a muddler or spoon to mash everything together.

5 Add the crushed ice to the glass.

6 Add the rum to the glass.

7 Fill the glass with club soda, stir and serve.

TASTING NOTES

You can order a mojito in the midst of a snowstorm in Bergen these days, but the Platonic ideal is served in Cuba, or Miami, home of the largest Cuban population outside of Cuba and stepping stone for the drink's transition to the modern cocktail scene.

Be it sweaty bar accompanied by the sound of song on a scratchy radio or a flash lounge, in any location, a good mojito is a wonderful twist on the tropical drink – cool, clear and refreshing, the mint and soda providing a zingy counterbalance to the heavy sugars of the rum. ● *by Adam Karlin*

KABOB

ORDER HERE

PIÑA COLAD

NO RUM $1.75
The Best
WITH RUM $2.00

THE BEST
Puertorrican
PIÑA COLADA

ORIGINS

Legend has it a 19th century pirate king invented a coconut cream and pineapple drink, but the old scallywag didn't leave the recipe. While it's indisputable that the piña colada we know today was invented in the glamorously popular Puerto Rico in the 1950s or 60s, the Caribe Hilton Hotel bar and Barrachina Restaurant hotly vie for the distinction of true originator.

SERVES 1

PUERTO RICO

PIÑA COLADA

The drink that practically begs to be sipped out of a coconut shell on a tropical sandy beach – accompanied, of course, by a paper umbrella.

YOU'LL NEED

60ml (2fl oz) cream of coconut (note: not coconut cream)
120ml (4fl oz) unsweetened pineapple juice
60ml (2fl oz) white rum or coconut milk
crushed ice
pineapple slice, to garnish
1 paper umbrella

METHOD

1 Pour cream of coconut, pineapple juice and white rum (or coconut milk) into a blender over crushed ice.

2 Blend, pour and serve.

3 Garnish with fresh pineapple slice and paper umbrella.

TASTING NOTES

Sweet and creamy coconut. Tangy pineapple juice. A healthy swig of rum. The piña colada, more than almost any other drink, calls to mind sunburned shoulders and warm tropical breezes. The sweetened coconut cream mellows out the bite of the pineapple and rum into a smoothie-like dessert drink. Taste-test for yourself next time you visit Puerto Rico (where piña coladas are the national drink). Both locations mentioned left still serve up their variation on the 'original' recipe. A virgin version is just as delicious: just add in a little more cream of coconut or coconut milk in place of the rum. ● *by Alex Leviton*

ORIGINS

Australia's wildest state has a long association with rum, dating from early colonial days when it passed as *de facto* currency. Since the late 1800s when explorer Henry Judd popularised hiking in Tasmania's wilderness, generations of bushwalkers have fortified themselves with this warming drink. Nowadays chocolate powder replaces the original cocoa, and milk powder is favoured over condensed milk.

SERVES 1

TASMANIA, AUSTRALIA

TASMANIAN BUSHWALKER'S RUM HOT CHOCOLATE

After hiking endless miles through frozen knee-deep mud at the end of the earth, nothing has a more soul-thawing effect than a steaming mug of hot chocolate laced with rum.

YOU'LL NEED

1 billy of water (a billy is a cylindrical pot used to boil water on a stove or fire)

3 sporks premium Italian chocolate powder (a spork is a popular bushwalking utensil combining both spoon and fork, equivalent to approx. 1 tbsp)

3 sporks (3 tbsp) milk powder

1 capful dark, underproof rum (locals prefer Bundaberg, for its lightweight plastic flask, but any rum will do)

METHOD

1 Boil the billy of water over a stove or open fire.

2 Add equal measures of chocolate and milk powders to your mug. You may need to adjust quantities depending on mug size.

3 Add boiled water and mix thoroughly with your spork to avoid clumping.

4 Add the rum and adjust to taste – a second capful may be be added, for medicinal reasons of course.

5 Hold mug in both hands close to face and sip.

6 Ignore rain on roof of hut or tent.

TASTING NOTES

It's getting dark, blowing a gale and you're soaked through as you finally reach the hut. Inside, your breath ghosts across the room and your head torch makes crazy shadows as you strip off, leaving puddles on the floor. Your mate cranks up the stove. By the time you're in dry clothes, they thrust a steaming mug into your hands. The seductive aroma of chocolate and alcohol caresses your senses. It's way too hot but you take a big gulp, scorch your mouth and fall into a blissful coma. While best enjoyed in a cosy mountain hut, you can also make this at home. Just stand under a cold shower first. ● *by Steve Waters*

WHISKY

When one engages in the time-honoured practice of offering someone a drink when they enter the home, it is commonly understood that the 'drink' will be whisky, or some variant thereof. That is the power of this spirit, at least in the Anglophone world – it is the alcohol signified by 'drink' in both pronoun and verb incarnation. And in that vein, whisky's flavours are the qualities millions associate with the concept of spirits. The experience of whisky – smoke, fire, wood, soil – is, for many, the essence of what a good drink is. →

DID YOU KNOW?

The age of a whisky is determined exclusively by time spent in cask barrels. If a whisky dates from the 19th century, it's not necessarily better than a whisky currently sitting on a store shelf – it all depends on barrel, not bottle ageing.

HISTORY

Whisky is liquor distilled from a grain mash, and the earliest records of such distillation trace back to the 12th century. Mentions of the 'water of life' - *uisce* in Gaelic, anglicised to 'whisky' later – date back to the 15th century in Ireland and Scotland. Although the drink was enjoyed recreationally, it was medicine as well; in Ireland, knowledge of distillation was passed between the Guild of Surgeon Barbers for years. Early excise taxes were levied on whisky distilleries, and as such some of the first tax revolts were fought over the spirit.

VARIANTS

First: 'whiskey' is what folks in the USA and Ireland drink. It's whisky everywhere else in the world. Scotch whisky is made in Scotland from malted barley, and comes in five varieties, ranging from single malt to blended.

In colonial America, corn was used over wheat as a distillation base, and whisky that is at least 51% corn is considered bourbon. Bourbon comes from Kentucky, but Tennessee also produces a bourbon commonly marketed as Tennessee Whiskey. The high sugar content in corn makes bourbon noticeably sweeter compared to its British Isle counterparts.

Another North American variant is rye whiskey. In the USA, rye whiskey must be distilled from at least 51% rye, but the Canadian version may not include rye at all. The flavour of American rye whiskey falls between the smokiness of Scottish and Irish spirits and the sweetness of bourbon.

Other big-hitters in the whisky-producing world include Japan and Tasmania.

TASTING

A proper whisky tastes like the essence of smoke, soil and fire. Done right, it's something like the feeling of a rainy day in Scotland or Ireland, or more accurately, being inside by a fire on a rainy day in Scotland or Ireland. It's cosiness you can drink.

Consume said drink from a wine or sherry glass. Take a deep nasal breath and feel the nose – the smells and all they evoke – settle on your brain. Let a sip sit on your palette for 20–30 seconds, then add some water to open up new flavour dimensions. ● *by Adam Karlin*

ORIGINS

According to legend, French–Canadian *voyageurs* (fur traders) concocted this winter warmer from a mix of whiskey and caribou blood, naming the drink after the reindeer-like beast that lives in Canada's north. These days sherry, port or sometimes red wine are the preferred mixers to blend with the harder alcohol. In Quebec province, you can buy Caribou premixed by the bottle. No caribou-hunting required.

SERVES 4–5

QUEBEC, CANADA

CARIBOU

A popular drink at Quebec City's Winter Carnival, this boozy Canadian beverage will make you forget all about the cold with its brawny blend of brandy, vodka, sherry, and port.

YOU'LL NEED
45ml (1½fl oz) brandy
45ml (1½fl oz) vodka
120ml (4fl oz) sherry
120ml (4fl oz) port
1 cinnamon stick (optional)

METHOD
To serve warm
1 Gently heat the brandy, vodka, sherry, port, and cinnamon stick in a medium saucepan.

2 Remove the cinnamon stick, then pour liquid into cups and serve.

To serve cold
1 In a punch bowl, mix the brandy, vodka, sherry, and port.

2 Fill four rocks glasses with ice, then divide the Caribou between the glasses, and serve.

TASTING NOTES
Quebec City's annual Winter Carnival mocks the frigid weather every February with snow sculptures, parades, parties and other festivities – and of course, the traditional Caribou drink. Caribou can be served chilled or warmed like a mulled wine, spiced with cinnamon. With its mix of booze and fortified wine, this alcoholic punch packs a punch, and warms you up. Many revellers pour their drinks into 'Bonhomme canes', hollow canes topped with the head of Bonhomme, the carnival's snowman mascot. Simply unscrew the head when you want to take a drink! ● *by Carolyn B. Heller*

ORIGINS

It was a stormy night in winter '43: a Canada-bound seaplane departing from Foynes port in south-west Ireland was forced to turn back due to foul weather. Chef Joe Sheridan greeted the chilled passengers with coffee laced with Irish whiskey, and a tradition was born. And in 1952, travel writer Stanton Delaplane was wowed by the drink at Shannon airport and took the secret home to America with him.

SERVES 1

SHANNON, IRELAND

IRISH COFFEE

**A balanced blend of caffeine and alcohol, Irish coffee
warms you up from the inside out. No wonder it's popular
in both rainy Ireland and foggy San Francisco.**

YOU'LL NEED

60ml (2fl oz) double cream
100ml (3½fl oz) hot strong
  coffee
2 tsp brown sugar
40ml (1½fl oz) Irish whiskey
fresh nutmeg (optional)

METHOD

1 Pour some hot water into the glass, just to warm it.

2 With a whisk, gently beat the cream until just thick but not
fluffy – it should still slide off a spoon.

3 In a separate glass, combine the coffee, sugar and whiskey
and stir until the sugar is dissolved.

4 Empty the hot water from the glass, then add the coffee
mixture. Gently spoon the cream over the coffee, in a thick
layer that fills the glass to the rim. (Some people prefer to
'float' the cream by pouring it gently over the back of a spoon.)

5 Grate nutmeg over the top, if desired.

TASTING NOTES

The first sip of a perfectly crafted Irish coffee is a marvel of sensations: first cold,
thick cream and perhaps the scent of nutmeg, then hot, sweet coffee, and finally
the gentle warmth of Irish whiskey. It tastes best in a wood-panelled pub or otherwise cosy
bar, ideally with a view of the nasty weather you're avoiding outside.

Irish coffee is a sort of magic trick in a glass, as the sugar in the coffee enables it
to support the cream. Avoid serving it in a straight-sided mug, as the cream will dissolve
too quickly. ● *by Zora O'Neill*

ORIGINS

One often-told story pinpoints the birthplace of this cocktail at the Manhattan Club of New York City in the 1870s. But one bartender of the time claimed the drink was created back in the 1860s by a Broadway bartender named Black. Whatever the truth, by 1900, the drink was a smash hit and today it remains an icon – one of the classics that every bartender worth his or her salt knows how to make.

SERVES 1

USA

MANHATTAN

Complex, elegant and timeless, the Manhattan is quite simply one of the world's great cocktails. A finely crafted version goes down smoothly and lingers on the palate. This is one to savour.

YOU'LL NEED
orange peel
60ml (2fl oz) rye whiskey
30ml (1fl oz) sweet vermouth
2 dashes of Angostura bitters
ice
maraschino cherry

METHOD
1 Rub the orange peel around the rim of a chilled v-shaped cocktail glass.

2 Put the rye, vermouth and bitters into a cocktail shaker.

3 Add ice and stir (don't shake).

4 Pour mixture through a strainer into the glass.

5 Add maraschino cherry. Enjoy.

TASTING NOTES
The ingredients seem deceptively simple: vermouth, bitters and rye whiskey (some use bourbon), but when properly constructed, the Manhattan is a finely balanced work of art. The bold and rich rye harmonises with the sweetness of vermouth and the sharp zing of bitters, making every sip a near transcendent experience – particularly when imbibed in a cocktail lounge in New York City. There's old-time jazz playing, a garrulous crowd lit by flickering candles, and a dexterous barkeep mixing up amber-hued cocktails behind a mahogany bar. The vibe, like the cocktail, is pure Manhattan: classy and seductive, with a dash of nostalgia. It's the start of a night that holds limitless possibilities. ● *by Regis St. Louis*

ORIGINS

While the exact history of the mint julep is unknown, it's thought to have originated in the Southern United States in the 18th century. Back then, doctors prescribed juleps for stomach aches and Virginians reputedly drank them for breakfast – those were the days! Although mint juleps were once made with spirits such as cognac or gin, the bourbon-based version has become the most popular.

SERVES 1

SOUTHERN UNITED STATES

MINT JULEP

Perfect for cooling down on hot, languid days, the mint julep – crushed ice crowned with zesty mint and spiked with bourbon – is an American classic.

YOU'LL NEED

20 mint leaves, plus an extra
   sprig of mint
60ml (2fl oz) bourbon
15ml (½fl oz) sugar syrup
crushed ice

METHOD

1 Gently bruise the mint in the palm of your hand to release its aroma. Place it in a chilled short tumbler or a julep cup.

2 Add bourbon and sugar syrup and stir gently.

3 Fill the glass with crushed ice and stir until the glass is frosted.

4 Top with more crushed ice if needed, garnish with the mint sprig and serve.

TASTING NOTES

Perhaps no other drink is as strongly associated with a sporting event as the mint julep, drunk to the sound of thundering hooves during the Kentucky Derby. About 120,000 are drunk over the two-day period of the Kentucky Oaks and the Kentucky Derby each year, when dressed-to-impress socialites and party-going punters alike mill about clutching frosty glasses, the sharp scent of mint filling the air. Can't get to the Derby? Sit on a shaded verandah on the hottest day of the year, fan your face with a broad-brimmed hat and slowly sip a julep. As the ice melts, it dilutes the bourbon, bringing out its vanilla and oak notes; the mint enlivens the palate right to the last delicious drop. ● by Luna Soo

ORIGINS

The Sazerac is credited to Antoine Amedie Peychaud, a New Orleans apothecary who served up homemade bitters, cognac and absinthe as a treatment for digestive problems in the 1830s. Decades later, absinthe was banned and cognac production dropped due to a grapevine pest devastating crops, but the Sazerac lived on, with whiskey and anise-flavoured Herbsaint instead of cognac and absinthe.

SERVES 1

NEW ORLEANS, USA

SAZERAC

Home to jazz greats and Mardi Gras, New Orleans is a heady combination of history and hedonism – and so is the city's official drink, the bold yet elegant Sazerac.

YOU'LL NEED

5ml (1tsp) absinthe or
   Herbsaint
60ml (2fl oz) cognac, rye
   whiskey or bourbon
15ml (1½fl oz) sugar syrup
3 dashes Peychaud's Bitters
ice
strip of lemon zest, pith
   removed

METHOD

1 Swirl the absinthe around the inside of a well-chilled short tumbler to coat. Discard any excess absinthe.

2 Add the cognac, rye whiskey or bourbon, sugar syrup and bitters to a separate glass. Fill with ice and stir with a bar spoon until the drink is ice-cold.

3 Strain the drink into the absinthe-coated old-fashioned glass.

4 Twist the lemon zest over the top (this will release the aromatic lemon oil into the drink) and drop it in to the cocktail as a garnish if you wish.

TASTING NOTES

After a day spent strolling through New Orleans' atmospheric French Quarter, a Sazerac is just the thing to kick off a big night in the Big Easy. As the sun sets on historic balconied buildings and saxophones wail into the sultry night air, settle in to a dive bar and order this potent cocktail, a well-balanced mix of spicy rye whiskey laced with medicinal aniseed that's best accompanied by a raucous jazz band and a lively crowd. Even those who don't like whiskey will enjoy a Sazerac's herbaceous scent and caramel undertones, and it's worth trying one with bourbon or cognac, too. Bourbon adds a fiery burnt-sugar note, while cognac makes a Sazerac smoother than the Nola bartender who convinced you to try all three. ● *by Luna Soo*

TASTING NOTES
The World's Best Drinks

TEQUILA

The fermented pulp of blue agave, distilled once or twice: defined this way, tequila almost sounds like a health drink. Unfortunately, thanks to youthful overindulgence, many people consider it quite the opposite. But quality tequila – the kind labelled '100% agave' rather than cheaper varieties filled with sugars – is one of the more richly flavoured and nuanced spirits the world has to offer. An inherently Mexican drink, one sip can conjure the spirit of a rowdy *cantina* and the sound of a *mariachi* serenade. →

117

HISTORY

Tequila was born in the 16th century when Spanish distilling techniques met the Aztecs' ritual agave-sap drink called *pulque*. The first registered manufacturer of the new liquor – called *mezcal*, referring to liquor made from any variety of agave – was the Cuervo family, in 1608, but it remained a somewhat raw product until it was refined for export in the late 19th century. This was also when the name was trimmed from mezcal de Tequila (the town that was, and still is, the centre of production) to simply tequila.

TASTING

Don't let the tiny glass fool you: good tequila is sipped, not slammed. Savouring it reveals a spicy, sometimes floral aroma and a sweet but multilayered flavour. This comes from the fact that *Agave tequilana* is, at its heart, a very large fruit: the piña, the pineapple-like core, takes a decade to develop its complex sugars and grow to its final weight, sometimes more than 200lbs (90kg).

Tequila's flavour varies according to where the agave is grown. Los Altos – the highlands northeast of Guadalajara – produces a sweeter, more delicate tequila, because the piña matures more slowly in the cooler air. In the lower elevations west of Guadalajara, around the namesake town of Tequila, you'll find intense, sometimes herbaceous spirits.

"GOOD TEQUILA IS SIPPED, NOT SLAMMED"

VARIANTS

Pure agave tequilas, usually about 40% alcohol, come in three main types:

Blanco (white) or *plata* (silver): Clear tequila, bottled immediately or up to two months after distillation.

Reposado (rested): Medium-gold tequila, aged up to a year in oak barrels.

Añejo (aged): Aged up to three years in small oak barrels, often formerly used for wine or whisky.

Agave's fruity notes are strongest in a *blanco*, although many aficionados prefer smoother *reposados*, especially for adding richness to a margarita. *Añejos* (and rarer three-plus-year-old *extra-añejos*) command a high price, but aren't necessarily better – many taste more like aged whiskies, as the agave flavour is overpowered by oak and char.

There are more than 900 tequila brands, but they all come from 100 or so distilleries in Jalisco state and areas of Michoacán, Tamaulipas, Nayarit and Guanajuato. To taste the widest range, check the NOM (Norma Oficial Mexicana) number on the seal to be sure you're buying from different distilleries.

● *by Zora O'Neill*

DID YOU KNOW?

Caballitos, the traditional thin tequila glasses, derive their shape from their original material, the tip of a bull's horn. These so-called *cuernitos* (little horns) supposedly changed names when a worker in an agave field told his boss that his tequila and shot glass weren't for him, but for his horse.

ORIGINS

Nobody agrees on who inspired the Margarita. Was it a dancer in 1938 Tijuana with allergies to all other spirits? Or Margarita Cansino, aka actor Rita Hayworth? Most likely the muse is prohibition drink, the Daisy, tweaked to use tequila instead of brandy. After all, the Spanish word for 'daisy' is *margarita*. In any case, it was Mariano Martinez's 1971 frozen Margarita machine that really inspired a taste for the drink.

SERVES 1

MEXICO

MARGARITA

A sip of Margarita captures the life and colour of a Mexican fiesta with lip-smacking lime and salt starting the party before the tequila dances in, all going down with the crushed-iced coolness of summer.

YOU'LL NEED

1 lime
a little salt on a plate
½ tsp fine sugar (optional)
20ml (¾fl oz) fresh lime juice
  (or other juice)
50ml (1¾fl oz) tequila
  (preferably *reposado*)
30ml (1fl oz) triple sec (eg
  Grand Marnier or Cointreau)
ice (optionally crushed)

METHOD

1 Prepare a chilled cocktail glass by running the juice from a lime wedge around the rim, then upturning the glass onto a plate of salt.

2 In a cocktail shaker, mix the sugar (if you want it sweet) in the lime juice (or other juice) until as dissolved as possible.

3 Add the tequila and triple sec, fill with ice (or crushed ice) and shake well.

4 Strain into the cocktail glass and decorate with a slice of lime.

TASTING NOTES

On balmy evenings with the music of both waves and *mariachi* crashing in, the first sight of the glittery rim of a Margarita glass is a fine moment. The citrus and salt carry the fragrance of a fresh sea breeze. Take your first sip and these sour and salty flavours cut through the sweetness of the orange liqueur and whatever other juice flavours you have chosen – perhaps tamarind, lychee or simply lemon. You know that tequila smokiness is there but it's soothed under crushed ice, making it all too easy to glug down before it kicks in and you have a sudden urge to leap up and move your hips. ● *by Phillip Tang*

© TIM E WHITE

ORIGINS

Credit for the Paloma usually goes to Don Javier Delgado Corona, of La Capilla in the town of Tequila, a no-frills *cantina* that nonetheless lands on many world's-best-bars lists. This is due to the charming don Javier himself, who at last check was in his 90s and still mixing drinks. Sure, there is another vague origin story, related to the 1860s folk song 'La Paloma' and then there's the Salty Chihuahua, a variant of the vodka-based Salty Dog, that's exactly the same as a Paloma. But let Don Javier have this – he's earned it.

SERVES 1

MEXICO

PALOMA

More commonly ordered in Mexico than the Margarita, the Paloma is a grapefruit-tequila combo that's just as refreshing as its lime-based cousin, with the perk of being much easier to make.

YOU'LL NEED

1 lime
cocktail salt
ice
60ml (2fl oz) tequila
 (preferably *blanco*)
30ml (1fl oz) grapefruit juice
30ml (1fl oz) club soda
sugar syrup or honey
 (optional, to taste)

METHOD

1 Run a lime wedge lightly around the rim of a tall (Collins) glass and dip into the salt.

2 Add ice to the glass, then tequila, grapefruit and soda. If the grapefruit is overly sour or bitter, adjust with sugar syrup or honey.

3 Stir gently and garnish with lime.

TASTING NOTES

The Paloma is simple: grapefruit juice and tequila, over ice in a salt-rimmed glass. Some add club soda; some dispense with the salt; some swap in Squirt or another one of Mexico's all-sugar-sweetened grapefruit sodas. All in all, it's a drink that's crisp, a little bitter, a little sweet and a great showcase for the uniquely Mexican flavour of tequila. Sipped in a ceiling-fan-cooled *cantina* or outside under a shady portal overlooking a plaza, it's perhaps the most elegant way to get a shot of tequila into your system. This recipe is the 'fancy' version – feel free to substitute grapefruit soda, though do try to find a sugar-sweetened one, which gives the drink the proper bite. ● *by Zora O'Neill*

ORIGINS

Allegedly, Sangrita was born when thrifty drinkers poured off the juices from a bowl of a Guadalajara-style fruit salad called *pico de gallo*, seasoned with salt, lime and ground hot *piquín* chiles. Although Sangrita was little known outside the state of Jalisco until later in the 20th century, it has since spread across most of the country.

SERVES 4

MEXICO

SANGRITA

Forget the lime and salt: in Mexico, a shot of tequila is traditionally served with a matching glass of this juice combo that's sweet, sour, spicy – and blood-red.

YOU'LL NEED

90ml (3fl oz) fresh-squeezed orange juice
90ml (3fl oz) pomegranate juice
60ml (2fl oz) tomato juice
2 tbsp Valentina hot sauce (or more, to taste)
pinch of salt

METHOD

1 Combine all ingredients and chill.

2 When ready to serve, taste again and balance flavours as necessary.

TASTING NOTES

Sangrita recipes abound. Purist bartenders mix citrus – sometimes including bitter Seville oranges – and pomegranate juice, plus ground chilli. A busy *cantina* may prefer the ease, speed and extra nourishment of tomato-based concoctions with ready-made hot sauce. Worcestershire sauce, grated onion and grenadine syrup all have their fans.

Regardless, each sip of Sangrita should have a balance of sweet and savoury, sour and hot. It should have body, but not be too thick – the goal is to clear and stimulate the palate, not coat it. It's typically served alongside tequila *blanco*, the clear, unaged spirit, which can still have a bit of a burn. The fruit juice tempers this, while complementing the tequila's natural sweet-spicy notes.

This recipe combination employs tomato juice for body and is more typical of what you'd find in a Mexico City bar. For extra national pride, serve this as a *Bandera*: one shot each of Sangrita, tequila and lime juice, a combination that mimics the red, white and green of the Mexican flag. ● *by Zora O'Neill*

AT THE BACK OF THE
SPIRIT
CABINET

We all know the drill: returning from a far-flung trip with a bottle of the country's local tipple, a souvenir of your travels and a happy reminder of long and lazy days soaking up a new culture (and its most quaffable produce). But months later, when that post-travel glow has faded and normal life resumed, there sits your spirit bottle upon the shelf, unopened and unloved.

Well, pull it out, dust it off and crack it open: it's time to be transported to those far-off lands again. →

ORIGINS

No one knows the exact origins of this Andean-style hot toddy. For locals in Quito, Bogotá and northern Peru, *canelazo* has always been consumed and is an intrinsic part of highland culture. At Christmas and during festivals, street vendors sell cups of *canelazo* from steaming cauldrons along the streets. It's perfect for warming up when out watching parades, or fireworks over cold mountain towns.

SERVES 4

THE ANDES

CANELAZO

On those chilly Andean nights, locals keep warm over steaming cups of *canelazo*, a citrusy, cinnamon-scented rum drink sold in highland towns. It's the perfect pick-me-up when temperatures plummet.

YOU'LL NEED

720ml (24fl oz) water
400–600g (16–24oz) brown
  sugar
juice of 2 limes
6–8 cinnamon sticks
1 tsp cloves
240ml (8oz) juice (orange,
  naranjillo or passion fruit)
120–240ml (4–8fl oz)
  aguardiente

METHOD

1 Put the water, sugar, lime juice, cinnamon sticks and cloves together in a large saucepan.

2 Bring to a boil, then lower heat and simmer for 30 minutes.

3 Remove from heat and add the juice and aguardiente.

4 Put back on stovetop and heat until warm and steaming.

5 Enjoy!

TASTING NOTES

True to its name *canelazo* (which comes from the Spanish word *canela*, meaning cinnamon) has a strong aroma of cinnamon. This is perhaps the first thing you note as you draw a hot cup of freshly-poured *canelazo* to your lips. Then you take a sip, and the sweetness of citrus (naranjillo, orange or passion fruit juice is used as a base) blends with the piquancy of cinnamon; then the kick arrives, courtesy of aguardiente (a clear, sugar cane-distilled rum), all of which combines for maximum refreshment during a frigid evening in a place like Quito's La Ronda district. On weekend nights, as live music spills out of colonial buildings along the frosty, cobblestone streets, the *canelazo* vendor is everyone's best friend. ● *by Regis St. Louis*

ORIGINS

Brazilians aren't too sure about the origins of their beloved cocktail, but speculation says it began life as a potent potpourri of lime, garlic and honey intended for Spanish flu sufferers, with rum added to expedite the therapeutic effects. Today, it certainly expedites something, but its medicinal effects would surely be limited to liquid courage (though some still believe it helps a common cold).

SERVES 1

BRAZIL

CAIPIRINHA

Put a little Brazil in your mouth! Sugary, sexy and simple, Brazil's national cocktail, a tantalising three-ingredient taste of tropicalia, goes down oh so sweet and easy. Blame it on Rio!

YOU'LL NEED

1 large lime
2 tbsp refined sugar
60ml (2fl oz) cachaça
crushed ice
sprig of mint

METHOD

1 Cut up the lime into four wedges, cutting around and discarding the core.

2 Place the wedges in the bottom of a rocks glass and muddle them for 15 seconds with the sugar.

3 Add crushed ice up to the rim of the glass.

4 Add cachaça and shake thoroughly in a cocktail shaker for 10-15 seconds.

5 Pour, garnish with the sprig of mint, and enjoy.

TASTING NOTES

A caipirinha is as sinister as it is simple: fresh limes and spoonfuls of sugar are drowned in cachaça, a sugar cane-distilled spirit native to Brazil and similar to rum, along with crushed ice. Nothing more, nothing less. The end result is a sickly-sweet and potent cocktail that goes down like candy. Variations can include caipiroska, made with vodka instead of cachaça; and caipifruta, made with a mix of various fruits rather than lime. You will also see versions made with tangerine, kiwi, star fruit, passion fruit – pretty much any fruit that tastes nice will taste even nicer when you throw sugar and alcohol at it! But the traditional recipe remains the most popular and ubiquitous in Brazil, an endless source of national pride. ● *by Kevin Raub*

ORIGINS

This aromatic aperitivo has been mixed since the 1930s. It is named after Giuseppe Garibaldi, the 19th-century politician and general who paved the way for Italy's unification. Fittingly, the recipe unites north and south Italy: Campari from Milan, and juice squeezed from Sicilian oranges. Paler siblings of the Garibaldi are served across Europe. But in a drink paying homage to the bold exploits of Giuseppe, weak colour won't do.

SERVES 1

ITALY

GARIBALDI

A Garibaldi is more than a blend of fresh orange and Campari. With each sip of this zesty aperitivo, you're toasting one of modern Italy's founding fathers.

YOU'LL NEED

3–4 blood oranges
3–4 ice cubes
60ml (2fl oz) Campari
1 slice of orange, to garnish

METHOD

1 Halve the fruit and reserve a thin slice of orange for the cocktail's garnish.

2 Squeeze the juice from the orange halves.

3 Tip the ice cubes into a highball glass.

4 Pour the Campari and about 150ml (5fl oz) of blood orange juice over the ice.

5 Adorn the rim of the glass with an orange slice and enjoy.

TASTING NOTES

The ruby hue of a well-mixed Garibaldi is thanks to a generous ratio of Campari to juice, and blood oranges. Freshly squeezed blood orange juice has an unmistakeable tart sweetness; it lends the Garibaldi essential piquancy. The first sip can shock the taste buds, but Campari's floral notes mellow the acid tang.

Sanguinello (blood orange) is a quintessentially Sicilian flavour – more than half of the island's orange groves are devoted to these distinctive citrus fruits. Many are cultivated near the slopes of Mount Etna, Europe's tallest active volcano. With its major ingredient blooming from volcanic soil, the Garibaldi has a fiery origin entirely suited to Italy's formidable founding father. ● *by Anita Isalska*

ORIGINS

No one knows who first struck upon the idea of soaking bread in water, adding some yeast and waiting for it to ferment. But what is certain is that Slavic peoples have been drinking kvas since at least the Middle Ages. It was commonly consumed during Peter the Great's reign, and enjoyed wide popularity during the Soviet days, when *kvas* was sold out of big yellow barrels. You can still see them in towns beyond the big cities.

MAKES 10 LITRES

RUSSIA

KVAS

On a hot afternoon when the sun hangs high over the glittering domes of town, nothing quite refreshes like *kvas*, a naturally fermented drink made from bread that Russians and Ukrainians have been drinking for centuries.

YOU'LL NEED

10 litres water
450g (1lb) of black, rye or
  brown bread
1½ tbs of dry yeast
800g sugar

METHOD

1 Put the water into a stockpot and bring to a boil. While water is heating, toast bread (stale bread works best for kvas).

2 When water boils, remove from heat and add bread. Cover let stand overnight. On the second day, remove the bread.

3 Mix together the yeast and sugar and add to the stockpot. Cover and leave to stand at room temperature for another six to eight hours.

4 Using a strainer or cheesecloth, pour the kvas into containers (plastic bottles work best) and store overnight in the fridge. Enjoy!

TASTING NOTES

Kvas is synonymous with summertime. With those long hot days, *kvas* vendors arrive in droves, doling out the cold, slightly frothy beverage from sidewalk stands all across Russia, Ukraine and beyond. It may sound off-putting – it's made from rye or black bread, has a slightly sour tang and is poured from a spigot – but once you taste it, you're hooked. And with its low alcohol content (typically around 1%) and cheap prices (about 40 rubles, less than US$1), you can drink to your heart's content. *Kvas* enthusiasts also tout its health benefits – and with beneficial live bacteria in every glass they may be on to something.

While easy to prepare, *kvas* takes a few days to make from start to finish owing to the fermentation process. ● *by Regis St. Louis*

ORIGINS

Brazil sips the caipirinha. Mexico quaffs the Margarita. But until 2006, Nicaragua had no cocktail to call its own. That year, the country's major rum producer, Flor de Caña, sponsored a contest to create a national drink. The only requirement was that the beverage include rum. A 67-year-old doctor, Edmundo Miranda, concocted the winning cocktail, which is named after the macuá, a local tropical bird.

SERVES 1

NICARAGUA

MACUÁ

Though its history is short, this tropical refresher made from rum, guava juice, and lime has become a popular drink at the cafés and beaches around this Central American nation.

YOU'LL NEED
ice
45ml (½fl oz) rum
30ml (1fl oz) orange juice
30ml (1fl oz) guava juice
15ml (½fl oz) lime juice
10ml (2 tsp) simple syrup (see below)
orange slice or lime wedge, to garnish

METHOD
1 Fill a cocktail shaker half-full with ice.

2 Add rum, orange juice, guava juice, lime juice, and simple syrup.

3 Shake until well-blended.

4 Fill a tall cocktail glass with ice, and strain drink into the glass.

5 Garnish with an orange slice or lime wedge, and serve.

TIP *To prepare a simple syrup, combine equal volumes of water and sugar in a small saucepan. Heat over a medium heat, and stir until sugar dissolves. Cool. This will keep refrigerated for at least a month.*

TASTING NOTES
Nothing says 'holiday' more than a fruity drink. Whether you're sipping a macuá on your terrace, or in a Nicaraguan beach café, this tropical slightly-sweet rum-based punch will put you in a holiday state of mind. In Nicaragua, you'll find macuá around the country, from the buzzing outdoor bars along Granada's Calle La Calzada, to the Pacific pubs in San Juan del Sur, to the low-key resorts on the Corn Islands off the Caribbean coast. Starting with a smooth rum base, the macuá mixes the citrus flavours of orange and lime with the tang of guava juice. It's sweetened with simple syrup and served over ice. *Salud!*
● *by Carolyn B. Heller*

ORIGINS

Pisco was originally produced with grapevines brought to South America by 16th century Spanish settlers, and both Peru and Chile claim ownership over it: the pisco sour is both countries' national cocktail. The competition remains fierce: when Anthony Bourdain sampled the drink in both countries, a Peruvian newspaper proudly reported that the famous chef preferred the local version.

SERVES 1

PERU & CHILE

PISCO SOUR

Tangy, sweet, and citrusy, the pisco sour – a cheerful grape brandy-based aperitif served chilled and practically glowing yellow – is like a lemon drop in a glass.

YOU'LL NEED

1 small lime (or ½ large lime),
   juiced
2 tbsp sugar
60 ml (2fl oz) pisco
1 tbsp egg white
ice
Angostura bitters

METHOD

1 Combine the lime juice and sugar in a blender until the sugar is fully dissolved.

2 Add the pisco, egg white and ice.

3 Pour into a glass, add a few drops of bitters and serve immediately.

TASTING NOTES

In any busy restaurant in Santiago or Lima, you'll notice waiters carrying trays laden with icy pisco sours – typically served in tall champagne flute-like glasses in Chile, and in shorter stemless glasses in Peru. While the cocktail is often paired with a savoury appetiser, the pisco sour is an aperitif that's meant to be started, and finished, before the main course is served. Refreshing but potent, the sugary sweetness offset by the sharp acidity of fresh lemon or lime, it's an ice-cold treat that opens the appetite for the meal to come. Raise your glass and take the first sip – don't be surprised if you're beckoning the waiter in short order to ask if the two-for-one happy hour special is still valid.

The preparation of a pisco sour is slightly different in Peru and Chile. In Peru, the cocktail is typically made with fresh lime juice and frothy egg white, while the Chilean version omits the egg white and employs fresh lemon juice. As a general rule of thumb, whether you're mixing drinks for one or for a crowd, the correct ratio for a pisco sour is 3:2:1, three parts pisco to two parts simple sugar to one part fresh lime or lemon juice. The recipe featured here is for a classic Peruvian-style pisco sour. ● *by Bridget Gleeson*

ORIGINS

Fermented millet beer has been
consumed by the Limbu people
of Nepal and northern India for
centuries, but the name *tongba*
actually refers to the lathe-
turned wooden pot the drink
is served in. The business end
of this intoxicant is technically
known as *jaand*, a fermented
mash of millet seeds and *marcha*, a traditional fermentation
starter, topped up with hot
water to liberate the flavours.

SERVES 20

EASTERN NEPAL, DARJEELING & SIKKIM

TONGBA

On a rugged Himalayan trek, nothing marks the end of a day on the trail quite like a hot pot of *tongba* – warming Nepali millet beer.

YOU'LL NEED

2kg (4lb 6oz) millet seed
5l (8½ pints) water
1 *marcha* cake (or to
   substitute, 4 oz of *koji*,
   available from Japanese
   supermarkets)
boiling water, for serving

METHOD

1 To make the *jaand* mash, the millet and water should be boiled together for two hours, then drained and mixed with the *marcha* (if you can find it), or *koji*.

2 Leave to ferment in an open bowl for four days, then pack tightly in a sealed, airtight jar and continue to ferment for a further two weeks.

3 To serve, add a cup of the *jaand* mash to your drinking vessel and top up with boiling water. Be sure to tightly seal the vessel containing your supply of *jaand* between servings to prevent the mash spoiling.

4 Allow your *tongba* to steep for five minutes before drinking. For authenticity, *tongba* should be served in a wooden *tongba* pot with a bamboo straw. If you don't have these, serve in a tankard, and sip through a squashed drinking straw.

TASTING NOTES

Sampling *tongba* is all about the setting. You should be exhausted from the day's trekking, huddled by a yak-dung fire to drive away the Himalayan cold. The walls should be lined with brass-bound wooden *tongba* pots. This is a drink that requires patience. The mash should stew for five minutes before you stick in the bamboo straw and sip the soul-warming millet beer inside. The flavour of *tongba* is that of the mountains: yeast, smoke and old timbers. In five minutes, you'll feel warm. In ten, you'll feel light-headed. A few more pots and you may fall over (alcohol is more effective at high altitudes!). ● *by Joe Bindloss*

NON-ALCOHOLIC DRINKS

It's not all about the hard stuff. There are times and places – when you're basking in the equatorial sunshine with an *água de coco*, say, or clearing the morning fug with a rich, frothy coffee, or sharing an American milkshake with the kids at a diner – when only a fresh and stimulating alcohol-free bevvie will cut it.

Soft drinks they may be, but don't be fooled: they can sure deliver a punch. →

ORIGINS

While residents of many tropical countries drink it, no one has the same passion for coconut water as Brazilians, who enjoy it on the beach, at markets and around town. As the world has learned of the health benefits of coconut water, its popularity has exploded, and today it's found on supermarket shelves everywhere. The boxed and pasteurised version, however, can't compare to a fresh serving straight from the fruit.

SERVES 1

BRAZIL

ÁGUA DE COCO

Whether you're lounging on a sun-kissed beach or simply refuelling after a long run, nothing satisfies quite like *água de coco* (coconut water), that deliciously sweet elixir perfected by nature.

YOU'LL NEED

a large, green coconut, preferably chilled

METHOD

1 Take a machete or large knife and make a straight cut off the top portion of the coconut.

2 When you see the white fleshy middle layer, cut out a triangular section to access the coconut water beneath.

3 Insert a straw and enjoy.

TASTING NOTES

The clear beverage is sweet and satisfying and mighty refreshing, particularly when it's served ice cold (*bem gelado* in Portuguese). At a kiosk overlooking Ipanema beach in Rio, the seller will take out a machete and hack away at the fruit, carving a small opening at the top. A straw (or two) will be inserted, and you'll be handed the fruit. That first sip conjures a sunny day in the tropics: palm trees, crashing waves and a long golden beach. It's both a great cap to the day (watching the sunset), or a fine start to the morning (many Brazilians swear by its hangover-curing properties). ● *by Regis St. Louis*

ORIGINS

Original versions of the milkshake were eggnog-like alcoholic drinks, but by the 1900s, the drink had become a healthy – wholesome maybe? – cold, flavoured-milk beverage. The invention of the blender early in the 20th century gave it the lighter-than-air consistency. And it's the solid cloud of whipped cream that gave us the iconic image of a cherry on top.

SERVES 1

USA

AMERICAN MILKSHAKE

Sweet, creamy, refreshing and comforting, the milkshake is the stuff of cherry-topped childhood dreams. Sitting at the counter of a diner, or maybe in a booth seat, a special family treat.

YOU'LL NEED

3 scoops of vanilla ice cream
60ml (2fl oz) chocolate syrup/ topping
360ml (12fl oz) full cream milk
120ml (4fl oz) whipped cream – canned for weird authentic experience, fresh for the gourmet take, but make sure it's the lightest whipped cream you've ever made!
1 maraschino cherry

METHOD

1 Place all the ingredients except the whipped cream and cherry into a jug – or better yet, a traditional metal milkshake cup. If you have a milkshake maker, it's time to plug it in. If not take out your trusty stick blender.

2 Blend the shake until it's well combined, but don't destroy the thick creaminess with over-blending.

3 Pour the shake into a tall milkshake glass and top with the whipped cream.

4 Carefully, precisely, place the cherry on top, exactly where you want it.

5 Serve with a straw and if you've made it well, you'll need a spoon too...

TASTING NOTES

It's time to get in touch with your inner child, the one you left sitting on one of those diner stools so long ago. We're heading down chocolate malt lane for this journey. And it has to be a diner. Find an American city – there'll be a diner. Don't be shy – go retro. Play a song on the jukebox. Sidle up to the counter. You know what to order. When it arrives, the bent candy-striped paper straw beckons. You take a sip and the rich warmth of chocolate hits you, but chilled milk doesn't let it become cloying: the cool, clean flavour just bring it all back home. Like you never left. ● *by Ben Handicott*

ORIGINS

Anijsmelk may well be a natural evolution of anise tea. The Dutch East Indies company (*Vereenigde Oost-Indische Compagnie* or VOC), founded in 1602 and once the largest spice trader in the world, imported Chinese star anise and Dutch women took to infusing their tea with this spice. Carrying the practice over to milk, a common drink thanks to the massive Dutch dairy industry, was clearly inevitable.

SERVES 1

THE NETHERLANDS

ANIJSMELK

Steamy warmed milk infused with delicate, licorice-flavoured anise showcases one of the Netherlands' signature flavours and its staple beverage, all in one soothing cup.

YOU'LL NEED

240ml (8fl oz) full fat milk
  (preferably unpasteurised)
1 heaped tsp anise seeds (or
  two or three pods of star
  anise may be substituted)
½ tsp sugar

METHOD

1 Bring the milk to a slow boil in a saucepan.

2 Slightly crush the anise seeds with the back of a spoon and add them and the sugar to the milk.

3 Turn the heat down and let the milk simmer for 10 minutes, stirring constantly so it doesn't burn.

4 Pour the milk into mug, straining through a fine sieve.

TASTING NOTES

When you're chilled by the North Sea winds after a canal skate or winter stroll through Amsterdam's cobbled streets, the Dutch provide a mug of steaming *Anijsmelk*, often served with *koek* (spice cake) or *olliebollen* (doughnuts). This winter warmer, traditionally offered to children, will give you a true sense of *gezelligheid*, a uniquely Dutch word best translated as a homeliness. *Anijsmelk*'s citrus-laced licorice fragrance pulls your attention as it wafts through the froth. Each creamy, sweet sip warms your insides as the anise, used as a cold remedy and digestive aid, envelopes you like a hug. ● *by Caroline Veldhuis*

ORIGINS

Ayran is at least a thousand years old. With no refrigeration, fresh milk was given a longer life by being made into yogurt; the addition of salt helped preserve it even longer, and made it more delicious. Ayran has long since become ubiquitous in Turkey – it's on the menu at McDonald's – though the city of Susurluk is especially renowned for its ayran, creamy but also delightfully foamy on top.

SERVES 4

TURKEY

AYRAN

Cut through summer heat and spicy food with this cold, salty yogurt drink. It's consumed all over the eastern Mediterranean – though Turkey takes special national pride in it.

YOU'LL NEED
500ml (16fl oz) yogurt
500ml (16fl oz) cold water
2 tsp salt (or more, to taste)
large pinch dried mint
  (optional)
6 ice cubes

METHOD
Combine all ingredients in a blender and blend until smooth and frothy. Alternatively, stir together yogurt, water, salt and the optional mint in a pitcher and pour over ice.

TASTING NOTES
You're a few bites into a spicy round of *lahmacun*, that snack of thin dough topped with ground meat. Or you've just polished off a few tender morsels of Adana kebab. What do you reach for to quench your thirst? The answer, any Turk will tell you, is ayran – in a hefty mug or from a bottle or foil-topped cup (shake both well, to froth them up). Ayran looks plain, but it works on many levels. The salt complements the meat. The dairy cools chilli heat. The yogurt critters help digestion. And, perhaps best of all, the sour flavour triggers your salivary glands and makes you dig back in to your meal.● *by Zora O'Neill*

ORIGINS

Sheer lore has it a colonial English gent disgruntled with the beverages of the region added milk and sugar to a rose water drink, but *bandung* is more likely an adaptation of Indian rose milk, featuring a flavour that also pays homage to Malaysia's Arabian and Persian influences. The artificial pink hue is thought to have been a marketing feature to distinguish it from *teh tarik*, a popular local milk tea.

SERVES 1

MALAYSIA & SINGAPORE

BANDUNG

Would a rose-flavoured drink by any other name taste as sweet and delightful? Ubiquitous and attention-getting, this bubble-gum pink refresher beckons travellers in Malaysia's sweltering heat and humidity.

YOU'LL NEED
ice cubes
120ml (4fl oz) evaporated milk
60ml (2fl oz) rose syrup
60ml (2fl oz) cold water
3–5 drops red food colouring

METHOD
1 Fill a tumbler ⅔ full of crushed ice.

2 Mix the evaporated milk and rose syrup in a separate glass and pour over ice.

3 Add water and stir.

4 Add red food colouring and stir.

TASTING NOTES
Loved equally as an everyday refresher and a mainstay of Malay festivities including weddings and Ramadan's nightly iftar feasts, bandung is found at hawker centres and chaotic street markets throughout Malaysia. Sitting in a restaurant and blinded by a fiery *laksa* or *rendang* (beef curry), you'll reach for the eye-popping *bandung* who proves she's more than just pretty, capably defusing the chilli-laden heat with an icy burst of floral sweetness. Don't drink too fast or you may get a head rush – linger over this veritable dessert in a glass to induce a sense of calm amidst the cacophony. ● *by Caroline Veldhuis*

KULS © 500PX

ORIGINS

Who said nothing good came out of the 1980s? In Taiwan, tea-lovers reinvented the humble cup of tea with the addition of boba – dessert-style balls of tapioca – creating an Asia-wide sensation. The prototype spawned a legion of hot and cold variations made with green tea, fruit tea, juices and even coffee. As the popularity of 'pearl milk tea' grew, so did the tapioca pearls, and the straws required to drink them!

SERVES 1

TAIWAN

BUBBLE TEA

Take one sweet, hot, caffeinated beverage and add instant fun! Soft, squishy balls of tapioca are the magic ingredient that transform pearl tea from workaday beverage into virtual dessert.

YOU'LL NEED

500ml (16fl oz) water
60g (2 oz) boba (large tapioca pearls, available from Asian supermarkets)
3 tbs sugar syrup (for preparing the *boba*)
1 teabag of your favourite tea
3 tbs canned sweetened condensed milk

METHOD

1 First prepare your tapioca pearls. Heat the water to a boil and slowly add the dry pearls.

2 Reduce the heat and stir gently until the pearls float to the surface. Simmer for 15 minutes on a medium heat, then allow to stand for 15 minutes.

3 Drain the pearls, mix with the sugar syrup, and set aside.

4 Next, prepare your tea the old-fashioned way, steeping a teabag in a cup of recently boiled, but not boiling, water. Set the tea aside in the fridge to chill.

5 To make your pearl tea, pour the chilled tea into a tall glass and stir in the condensed milk, then pour in your tapioca pearls. Serve with an outsized straw for slurping up the boba (or provide a long spoon).

TASTING NOTES

Bubble tea is not just a drink, it's an interactive game. You never know which sip will be sweet liquid tea, and which sip will deliver a sweet, sticky ball of tapioca. The giant straw is an integral part of the bubble tea experience, just large enough to accommodate a giant tapioca pearl. If you get lucky and slurp a pearl, you'll get the frisson of anticipation as the flow of liquid slows, before the pearl arrives suddenly, sweet and soft, in your mouth. If you like tapioca balls, look out for variants with grass jelly and balls of aloe, sago, taro root and egg pudding. ● *by Joe Bindloss*

ORIGINS

Like India and Sri Lanka before them, the highlands of East Africa were earmarked for tea plantations by British colonialists in the late 19th century. It wasn't long before tea drinking caught on, and as Indians experimented with adding a mixture of spices to their tea to create what became known as *masala chai*, East Africans looked to just one of them – cardamom – to give their cuppa a sweet, aromatic kick.

SERVES 4

EAST AFRICA

CARDAMOM TEA

The recipe and its ingredients may borrow from other lands, but East Africa has managed to fuse the cash crops of its colonists and the fruits of faraway traders into a hot drink that is uniquely its own.

YOU'LL NEED
700–1400ml (24–48fl oz)
  boiling water
3–4 tsp Earl Grey tea
6 green cardamom pods,
  bruised
milk, to taste
honey or sugar to sweeten,
  if desired

METHOD
1 Add the water, tea and lightly crushed cardamom pods to a saucepan and bring to the boil.

2 Add the milk, ideally enough to turn the mixture to a pale beige colour, and sweetener.

3 Bring the mixture to the boil again.

4 Take the saucepan off the heat and allow the mixture to steep for several minutes before straining and serving.

TASTING NOTES
When the humble cardamom pod was brought to East Africa by spice traders from the East Indies, it was embraced locally as the perfect way to add depth of flavour to the classic British brew with the added benefit of freshening breath, detoxifying the body and aiding digestion. These days, many 'African chais' blend cardamom with spices such as cassia, vanilla, nutmeg, ginger and cloves. But even on its own, the woody notes and citrusy (some say grapefruity) undertone of cardamom effortlessly manages to transform afternoon tea into an exotic adventure. ● *by Sarah Reid*

ORIGINS

The history of tea drinking in the subcontinent goes back 5000 years, but it was the British who were responsible for transforming a Chinese leaf infusion into the fermented, milky drink that people know and love today.
In a bid to break the Chinese tea monopoly, plantations were established in the hills of Assam, and the Indian Tea Association embarked on a massive campaign to popularise Indian tea worldwide. With this being India, people couldn't resist adding milk, sugar and a pinch of masala spices, and so chai was born.

SERVES 1

INDIA

CHAI

A shot-sized blast of sugary creaminess, chai is not just a cup of tea, it's the fuel of the Indian subcontinent!

YOU'LL NEED

1 tbs loose black tea
1 tbs granulated sugar
240ml (8fl oz) milk
120ml (4fl oz) water
1 cardamom pod
1 clove
1 small piece cinnamon stick
1cm piece of fresh ginger
2 whole black peppercorns

METHOD

1 In a small metal pan, mix all the ingredients and heat, stirring constantly.

2 Allow the mixture to froth up repeatedly to boil off some of the water and concentrate the tea. This should take about five minutes.

3 Once the tea is steeped, pour through a strainer into a cup or glass – be sure to pour from a height to aerate the mixture en route! Serve immediately.

TASTING NOTES

The location is an essential part of the chai experience. This is a drink to sip at dawn in front of a panorama of Himalayan peaks, or at dusk on a dusty railway station with the sun slowly sinking over the horizon. It will most likely be served in a tiny glass, beside a hissing kerosene stove, so you'll get to the see the whole ritual of pouring the drink from a distance, with a cocktail-maker's flourish. Then you get to taste: at first all you get is sugar and milkiness, before the pep of the tea leaves and the subtle flavour of the masala – cardamom, ginger, cinnamon, pepper, nutmeg and cloves – starts to seep through. Pow! Even if you were exhausted to the point of collapse by India's bustle and noise, you're awake now! ● *by Joe Bindloss*

ORIGINS

Cocoa (or cacao) is a contrary bean: it only feels comfortable in a narrow slither of humid, tropical land stretching 10 degrees north and south of the equator, often called the world's chocolate belt. St Lucia, which sits within this belt, is also blessed with an overflowing natural spice rack of nutmeg, cloves and cinnamon; little surprise, then, that chocolate and spice blend so effortlessly in this Caribbean take on hot chocolate.

SERVES 2

ST LUCIA

COCOA TEA

In the fertile gardens of St Lucia, plump cocoa pods can be swiped straight from the trees to make this rich chocolatey breakfast drink spiced with local nutmeg, bay leaves and cinnamon.

YOU'LL NEED

480ml (16fl oz) water
bay leaf
¼ tsp cinnamon
¼ tsp nutmeg
4oz grated Lucian cocoa stick
240ml (8fl oz) fresh,
  evaporated or powdered
  milk (or cream)
sugar, to sweeten
1 tbsp cornstarch
½ tsp vanilla

METHOD

1 Boil the water with the bay leaf, cinnamon and nutmeg; let it bubble for about 15 minutes.

2 Grate the cocoa stick into the boiling water and boil for another 10 minutes.

3 Add the milk (fresh, evaporated or powdered) and sweeten to taste. For a more luxurious taste, you could also try cream.

4 Mix the cornstarch with water and slowly add to the boiling mixture, stirring all the time.

5 Finally add the vanilla, then strain and serve.

TASTING NOTES

Imagine the exotic aromas of an Asian chai tea and then wrap a warm, velvety chocolate blanket around it. You won't find cocoa tea on the menu at any standard five-star Caribbean resort: this drink is for comfort slurping and for comparing to how mama used to make it. It's for bleary-eyed early mornings and for roadside pit-stops on the way to work. At breakfast stalls, you might catch a glimpse of the cocoa being infused with spices on a rough stove. Add a greasy *accra* (salt fish fritter, mixed with hot pepper and spring onion) or two and your morning is set up for success. ● *by Lorna Parkes*

ORIGINS

Coffee beans made their way
into a drink in 15th century
Yemen. Popularised in the early
20th century after the invention
of instant coffee, the gold
standard is espresso, made with
the steam machine invented
by Italian Angelo Moriondo in
1882. A significant development
in 20th century coffee culture
was the invention of the flat
white – a double espresso with
unfrothed milk – in New Zealand
in the late 1980s.

SERVES 1

WORLDWIDE

COFFEE

Coffee is one of the world's most popular drinks, pepped up with caffeine and packed with flavours ranging from fruit and nuts to chocolate and cinnamon.

YOU'LL NEED

1 tbsp medium-fine ground coffee, preferably from freshly roasted beans
30ml (1fl oz) water

METHOD

An easy and reliable method to make good coffee at home is the stovetop espresso 'moka pot' in which water is expressed through the grind. The quantities given here (see left) will provide one shot of espresso using a moka pot.

Beyond following the manufacturer's instructions, a tasty stovetop brew depends on taking it off the heat at the right time – coffee is prone to burn, so don't overcook it.

TASTING NOTES

Purists argue that proper coffee is best served black. Others believe the addition of milk enhances the flavour as does a sprinkle of sugar or chocolate. It's a personal thing, and necessarily so. Different beans exhibit a wide range of flavours, not only down to type and roasting technique but also *terroir* – the particular growing conditions. Fair Trade beans leave a better taste in the mouth.

The flavour and texture is enhanced by drinking it from the right cup, such as a demitasse for an espresso, and a tulip for a flat white. ● *by Sarah Bennett and Lee Slater*

ORIGINS

The original 19th century egg
cream may have contained an
egg, but a more likely explanation for the misleading name is
that 'egg' is a corruption of echt
(Yiddish for 'genuine'), and that
early sellers of this soda-foun-
tain concoction were advertising
'a genuine cream soda'. What all
egg cream lovers can agree on
is that the drink is as genuinely
New York City as Central Park or
the Brooklyn Bridge.

SERVES 1

NEW YORK, USA

EGG CREAM

A sweet, creamy cross between milkshake and soda, the egg cream contains neither eggs nor cream, making this time-honoured classic associated with Old New York as misleading as it is delicious.

YOU'LL NEED

60ml (2fl oz) whole milk
120ml (4fl oz) soda water,
   chilled
chocolate syrup (Fox's U-Bet,
   if you can get it)

METHOD

1 Fill a bell-shaped 8oz glass ¼ full with milk.

2 Add cold soda water, leaving about an inch of space at the top of the glass.

3 Using a long handled spoon, stir in the chocolate syrup to taste. The stirring should mix the milk, soda and syrup, creating a creamy foam head thick enough for a straw to stand straight up.

4 Enjoy! Life is short, and a genuine egg cream's fizz won't last long!

TASTING NOTES

New Yorkers are known for being particular, and the difference between a perfect and imperfect egg cream is best manifested in the creamy foam head (or lack thereof), inside of which there should be wispy traces of syrup. The best way to maximise the head is to serve the egg cream in a bell-shaped glass, with a wider top than bottom. The head should be thick enough to hold your straw straight up. As for syrup, chocolate and vanilla are the only echt choices. Purists, however, insist that vanilla is too posh a flavour for the beverage's working class roots, and that a true Brooklyn-ite wouldn't be caught dead drinking anything other than chocolate. Fistfights have broken out over the 'true way' to make an egg cream, with the main division concerning the syrup-adding stage. We've gone with the 'syrup last' method. ● *by Joshua Samuel Brown*

ORIGINS

Though a bottled version made by Manhattan Special has been available for ages, freshly made espresso soda is considered a trendy summer beverage, especially in the Pacific Northwest, where coffee drinking is serious business (Starbucks started in Seattle, after all) and exquisite caffeinated concoctions are developed, honed, then consumed with gusto by all.

SERVES 1

USA

ESPRESSO SODA

This strange stepchild of an Italian soda and iced coffee is trending in places where coffee aficionados pull shots of single-origin espresso while discussing the hand-versus-machine ground beans with great earnestness.

YOU'LL NEED

syrup, to taste (hazelnut, vanilla or almond all work well)
ice
240ml (8fl oz) soda water
30ml (1fl oz) half & half (or, if unavailable, cream or milk)
2 shots espresso or 60ml (2fl oz) of cold-brew coffee

METHOD

1 Put the syrup and ice in a 16-oz glass.

2 Add the soda water and half & half.

3 Add espresso/cold-brew coffee. The espresso and soda water should separate, creating a dual-layer effect with the espresso floating on top of the soda.

4 Mix and drink through a straw!

TASTING NOTES

A shot of espresso served with carbonated water seems a strange mix unless one considers that the humble Iced Americano, this exotic beverage's non-carbonated cousin, is a top-selling summer coffee cart beverage. What makes this drink exquisite is the syrup – vanilla, hazelnut or caramel work best – which, when blended with the espresso (or currently trending cold-brew coffee) and served over iced soda water, creates a carbonated, caffeinated taste sensation guaranteed to jolt your senses on a hot afternoon. Those who normally take their coffee drinks with cream will find the combination of cream, espresso, syrup and soda produces a fantastically fizzy beverage reminiscent of a grown-up New York egg cream. ● *by Joshua Samuel Brown*

ORIGINS

Beverages sold as *horchata* abound throughout Latin America, having first come from Spain (where it was – and still is – made from *chufa* nuts). *Horchata* in the New World leans closer to the Mexican version, made from ground rice or almonds, vanilla and cinnamon. Its popularity in cultures known for spicy cuisine should come as no surprise – *horchata* is an intestinal balm.

MEXICO & LATIN AMERICA

HORCHATA

MAKES A JUG FOR 6~10

Pronounced *or-CHA-tah*, this rice-milk drink is thirst-quenching, nutritious and the perfect counterbalance to the spiciness of Mexican and Central American cuisines. Some variations use milks derived from nuts.

YOU'LL NEED

200g (1 cup) uncooked long grain white rice
cinnamon stick or ½ tsp of ground cinnamon
1.2l (5 cups) water
200g (1 cup) white sugar
1 tsp vanilla extract

METHOD

1 Pulverise the rice using a blender or a (clean) coffee grinder until it's about the consistency of finely ground coffee beans.

2 Place the rice and cinnamon in a bowl, adding 750ml of warm water. Cover and allow to sit overnight (or even longer) at room temperature.

3 Pour the mixture into a blender or food processor. Blend until as smooth as possible.

4 Add 500ml cold water. Blend again.

5 Strain the mixture through a sieve lined with cheesecloth or a very fine strainer. You may have to clean out the rice gunk a couple of times as you go.

6 Transfer to a pitcher and mix in the sugar and vanilla extract until dissolved. Add more or less sugar to taste. (Honey and agave are both acceptable substitutes.)

7 Serve over ice with a dash of ground cinnamon.

TASTING NOTES

Your first sip of *horchata* may follow a bite of a spicy Mexican dish like *chile rellenos* (spicy peppers, stuffed and roasted). If so, the beverage's distinctly soothing properties – for which you will be grateful – will be the first thing you notice. As the culinary fires are quenched, the drink's milky sweetness, tinged with strong overtones of cinnamon and lighter notes of vanilla will move to the forefront. You may find the beverage reminiscent of rice pudding enjoyed as a child, making it all the more interesting as a counterpoint to your next bite of fiery Mexican food. ● *by Joshua Samuel Brown*

ORIGINS

The ancient Egyptians began malting barley for the precursor to beer possibly 4000 years ago. To 'malt' a grain means to allow it to start germinating, setting off the enzymatic process that converts starches to sugars. Before it fully sprouts, the grain is quick-dried. *Voilà*: malt! You might recognise the rich-tasting grain from commercial malted drinks like Ovaltine or Horlicks, or in malted chocolate balls.

SERVES 1

USA

MALTED MILKSHAKE

Beer might have given malt its most illustrious fame, but when mixed into a milkshake (or even waffles), the nutrient-rich, slightly sweet grain adds a level of delicious complexity.

YOU'LL NEED

3 tbsp warm water
1 tbsp unsweetened cocoa
  powder
1 tbsp whole milk powder
180 ml (6fl oz) vanilla ice
  cream
⅓ frozen banana, peeled and
  cut into small pieces before
  freezing
60 ml (2fl oz) milk
2 tbsp malted barley powder

METHOD

1 Dissolve the cocoa powder and whole milk powder in warm water, mix well.

2 Add the ice cream, frozen banana, milk and malt powder to a blender.

3 Pour the cooled cocoa mixture on top.

4 Blend, then serve.

TASTING NOTES

Beer and whisky connoisseurs recognise fermented malted grains as what gives the alcoholic beverages their rich sweetness. But unfermented malted grains can impart a distinct, earthy flavour to non-alcoholic drinks as well.

You can find a malted milkshake at an old-fashioned Main Street diner in Any Town, USA, or just mix Ovaltine or Horlicks with hot milk. You can also buy straight malted barley flour (available online or in high-end grocery stores) and add it to cakes, milkshakes or brownies. The heartiness of malt pairs especially well with cocoa. ● *by Alex Leviton*

ORIGINS

In India, lassi is as old as the hills, and those hills are very old indeed. According to ancient Ayurvedic texts, the people of the Indian Punjab have been mixing curds, sugar and water together as an aid to digestion for thousands of years. The addition of mango was a later piece of inspiration, invented to help take the heat out of the sweltering Indian summer. It's both tastier and more predictable than India's other famous lassi, made with *bhang* (marijuana).

SERVES 1

INDIA

MANGO LASSI

Forget milkshakes and smoothies; India's mango and yoghurt lassi was the original fruit sensation. This probiotic digestion aid has been a staple on Indian menus since at least 3000BC.

YOU'LL NEED

200g (1 cup) chopped fresh mango (ideally Alphonso mango)
100g (½ cup) thick natural yoghurt (full-fat Greek yoghurt is fine)
50g (¼ cup) water
2 tsp sugar

METHOD

1 Too easy. Combine the mango, yoghurt and sugar in a blender and add water, a little at a time, until the lassi reaches the required consistency. The mix should be thin enough to drink through a straw, but never watery.

2 For authenticity, used chilled fruit and yoghurt and serve immediately, rather than chilling your lassi afterwards in the fridge. Transportation to the Indian plains awaits...

TASTING NOTES

A lot of things don't survive the transition from travelling to back home. K-pop; hair-braids; Thai fishermen's trousers. Mango lassi is different. It's just as uplifting sipped at the gym as it is on a dusty train platform on the Indian plains. A lot will depend on the quality of your mangoes, however. Done right, a mango lassi should be thick, creamy and sweet – the flavour of an Indian summer afternoon – but still sippable: this is a drink remember, not a dessert. Look for subtle overtones of cardamom or rose water, often used alongside the tangy yoghurt, mango and sugar. ● *by Joe Bindloss*

ORIGINS

Saddling your camel at dawn to trek over the dunes, luxuriating in a lavish riad in Marrakech, watching the sun set over a kasbah or eating a tagine in Fez, you will be offered mint tea all day long. During the Crimean war in the 1850s, a British tea merchant could not offload his wares in the Balkans so was looking for other customers. It was love at first taste for Moroccans.

SERVES 2

MOROCCO

MINT TEA

Mint tea and Morocco go together like camels and the Sahara or carpets and Marrakech. Made from gunpowder tea, zingy spearmint and a LOT of sugar, it is the essence of Moroccan hospitality.

YOU'LL NEED
500ml (1 pint) water
2 heaped tsp gunpowder tea
6 sugar cubes
a handful of fresh spearmint
  sprigs, washed
sugar cubes, to taste

METHOD
1 In a metal teapot, bring the water to the boil.

2 Add the tea leaves and about six sugar cubes, and bring to the boil again.

3 Take off the heat and add the mint, then return to the boil.

4 Take off the heat and allow to brew for a few minutes.

5 Pour one glass of tea, then return it to the pot.

6 Pour the tea from a height to aerate it and to produce a crown of froth. Serve, with more sugar if required.

TASTING NOTES
While women are in charge of food, it is men who serve the tea, with great ritual. Spearmint, along with wormwood in winter or verbena for a lemony fragrance, are sold from carts in the *souk* and bought fresh at least once a day. Gunpowder tea leaves are put in an engraved silver teapot along with the mint and sugar, often broken off a large cone with a silver hammer. Glasses are set on a tray and the pot set on the heat to brew. The first glass of tea is examined and returned to the pot. The tea is poured from a great height so that a frothy 'crown' is produced. It is polite to drink three glasses. ● *by Helen Ranger*

ORIGINS

Hailing from the Thai-Chinese community, the name oliang derives from the Teochew dialect; the *o* part means 'black' while *liang* means 'iced'. This iced, black breakfast drink has stayed true to its roots and, while there are variations, it is usually found only on roadside stalls or in rustic restaurants, not in fancy coffee shops.

THAILAND

OLIANG

SERVES 4

Forget Starbucks; when it comes to starting the day with a real caffeine kick, the only thing that really hits the spot is a glass of sharp and bitter *oliang*, a traditional Thai-Chinese version of iced coffee.

YOU'LL NEED

2 tbs dried corn
2 tbs soybeans
1 tsp white sesame seeds
4 tbs coffee beans (robusta is best)
500ml (2 cups) boiling water
1 tbs sugar
500ml (2 cups) crushed ice

METHOD

1 Roast the corn and soybeans in a large frying pan on a low heat, shaking them occasionally. After about 5–8 minutes, when they start to brown, turn off the heat and add the sesame seeds.

2 Leave everything to cool completely, then stir in the coffee beans.

3 Transfer the mixture to a coffee grinder and process until it becomes powdery, or pound the mixture using a mortar and pestle if you don't own a coffee grinder.

4 Tip the powder into a large heatproof jug. Add the boiling water and leave to infuse for 1 minute.

5 Strain the liquid through a muslin or coffee filter into four heatproof coffee glasses and leave to stand for 5 minutes. If you only have thick standard glasses, place a metal teaspoon in each before adding the hot liquid, as this will prevent the glass from cracking.

6 Add the sugar and stir to dissolve. Add the crushed ice and serve immediately.

TASTING NOTES

For decades, *oliang* has been the drink of choice for Thais, who love its powerful, cool flavours. Imagine starting your day at a busy Thai restaurant, sitting on a blue plastic stool, surrounded by wooden tables and bare floors. Your *oliang* arrives, a glistening combination of ice, coffee and soybeans. Take a sniff first; it's coffee, but not as you know it. As you sip, the coffee flavours flood your senses, but they are quickly overtaken by the bitter notes of the soybeans. The aftertaste is wonderfully robust and sharp. ● *by Mark Beales*

ORIGINS

A form of root beer was being brewed by Native Americans long before Europeans arrived. The herbal concoction was used to soothe coughs and various ailments. Modern root beer became popular across the United States in the 1800s, but its place in American lore was cemented during 1920s Prohibition, when brewers turned their equipment to the closest non-alcoholic drink they were allowed to make.

SERVES 4

USA

ROOT BEER FLOAT

The refreshing, foamy carbonated soda is sweet yet complex, tailor-made for a humid summer evening. Toss in a scoop of ice cream for a real treat.

YOU'LL NEED

250ml (8fl oz) homemade root beer (see below), or use ready-made root beer
1 scoop vanilla ice cream

For homemade root beer
250g (8oz) white granulated sugar
¼ tsp baker's yeast
1 tbsp root beer extract
1.75 litres (60fl oz) water

2l (67fl oz) plastic bottle or glass beer growler, thoroughly cleaned funnel

METHOD

1 Place the funnel in mouth of bottle or jug. Be very careful with a glass jug, as over-carbonated root beer can explode.

2 Pour in the sugar and baker's yeast and shake bottle to thoroughly mix. Pour in the root beer extract and swirl the bottle gently until thoroughly blended.

3 Pour in the water and shake well until thoroughly mixed.

4 Cap the jug or bottle and place the bottle out of direct sunlight and allow to carbonate for 2–4 days.

5 Check after two days for carbonation. When carbonated, refrigerate and serve.

6 To make a root beer float, simply add a generous scoop of vanilla ice cream. Do not blend.

TASTING NOTES

Depending on who's doing the brewing, root beer can be filled with all manner of exotic flavours: anise, liquorice root, birch oil, vanilla, wintergreen, nutmeg, sarsaparilla, molasses, honey. (Its original ingredient, sassafras, was deemed a liver toxin and removed in the 1960s). The result is a complex blend of earthy flavours, punctuated by a spicy sweetness reminiscent of mint or liquorice. Commercial varieties exist, but artisanal root beer by craft brewers has now become popular. The brewing process requires speciality ingredients, but they are all available to buy online. ● by Alex Leviton

YOU'LL NEED

For the grenadine syrup
250ml (8fl oz) unsweetened
  pomegranate juice
250g (8 oz) white granulated
  sugar
1 tsp lemon juice
splash orange blossom water
  or rose water (optional)

For the Shirley Temple
ice
250ml (8fl oz) ginger ale,
  lemon-lime soda, or cola
1 tbsp grenadine syrup
maraschino cherry
wedge of lime, to serve

ORIGINS

Mixed drinks often have multiple
origin theories. The Shirley Temple – named for the eponymous
child actress – is no exception.
Legend says the exclusive
Chasen's LA restaurant invented
the 'mocktail' in the 1930s for
the precocious young star to
drink when out with her adult
co-stars. However, the adult
Shirley Temple-Black herself
said she thought the drink was
invented at Hollywood's Brown
Derby restaurant.

SERVES 4

USA

SHIRLEY TEMPLE

You don't have to be a boring old grown-up to get your very own fancy mock cocktail. Even better, this one comes complete with an accompanying maraschino cherry (or two).

METHOD

For the grenadine syrup

1 Bring the pomegranate juice to a boil over a medium heat. Turn down the heat and stir in the sugar.

2 Bring up the heat for 10–20 minutes, stirring to dissolve the sugar until mixture thickens slightly, being careful not to let it boil over.

3 Take off the heat and stir in the lemon juice (and optional splash of orange blossom or rose water). Let cool for 30 minutes.

4 Pour into a glass container and cover tightly. It will keep in the fridge for up to a month.

For the Shirley Temple

1 Fill a tall glass tumbler with ice cubes.

2 Pour in the ginger ale, lemon-lime soda, or cola.

3 Add a tablespoon of grenadine syrup to taste.

4 Top with a maraschino cherry and, if desired, a lime wedge.

TASTING NOTES

You're at one of those fancy restaurants. Grandpa Fred is knocking back a Negroni, Grandma Jane's nursing a vodka tonic on the rocks. What's a kid to order? Milk? Juice? Pshaw. That's for babies. Big kids drink a Shirley Temple. Or a Roy Rogers.

Refreshingly sweet, the flavour complexity comes from the grenadine syrup's fruity tone. Most commercial varieties are now made with high fructose corn syrup and artificial food colouring. To bring out the original pomegranate flavour, simply make your own grenadine syrup in 20 minutes. ● *by Alex Leviton*

ORIGINS

Americans lay claim to first 'naming' the smoothie, and some sources state that the Waring Blender company mentioned the term 'smoothie' in its cookbooks in the 1940s. Others say the word became the norm during the 'hippy sixties', when smoothies were offered as a healthy alternative to the popular milkshake as part of a new wave of macrobiotic vegetarianism.

SERVES 4

WORLDWIDE

BANANA SMOOTHIE

Smoothies are not a new treat; for centuries, people around the world have pureed local fruits with ice, milk, yoghurt or ice cream to create dense, satisfying beverages.

YOU'LL NEED

2 ripe bananas, peeled and
   roughly chopped
360ml (12fl oz) skimmed milk,
   chilled
1.7l natural yoghurt (full-fat or
   low-fat)
1 tbs honey
1 tbs wheatgerm

METHOD

1 Place the bananas, milk, yoghurt, honey and wheatgerm in a blender.

2 Process the mixture until it is well combined and smooth.

3 Pour the smoothie into four glasses.

4 Serve the smoothies immediately.

TASTING NOTES

The versatile drink's cream-like texture rolls like velvet across your tongue. Even your teeth get some post-taste action. And hey, you get to do it all over again, at least for as many gulps as it takes to finish this very satisfying and filling 'edible drink'. The best time to enjoy a smoothie is when you're hungry (rather than thirsty); it's a meal in itself.

There are more smoothie recipes than there are cookbooks. The banana smoothie is undoubtedly one of the classics (and ours has a healthy twist to boot). You can use any blendable fruit in place of bananas and supplement wheatgerm with superfoods such as chia seeds. ● *by Kate Armstrong*

TASTING NOTES
The World's Best Drinks

TEA

Let's get one thing straight from the off: we're not talking about teabags here. We're talking about quality Chinese single-estate loose-leaf tea. Tea that has been perfected by tea-growing experts over the course of more than 2000 years. It all comes from one plant – *camellia sinensis* – yet different soils, climates and production methods mean that it can be used to create thousands of different teas. Listen; you can almost hear the spring water – hot, but not quite boiling – trickling into the porcelain, tea leaf-filled *gaiwan* (lidded cup) that sits before you on its wooden tea tray in its courtyard teahouse. In a moment, the flowery fragrances of oolong will waft up from the table in front of you, signalling the approach of that most wonderful time of day: your first cup of tea.→

VARIANTS

Tea types differ according to the amount of oxidisation the tea leaves undergo during processing. This happens when enzymes in the leaves are exposed to the air after being picked, in the same way that an apple turns brown when cut. So lighter teas will have undergone almost no oxidisation, while dark teas will be almost fully oxidised. Oolongs fall somewhere in between. Post-fermented teas such as pu'erh, meanwhile, are teas (usually green) that are processed as normal, then left to ferment for many years in special storage rooms.

HISTORY

● **200BC:** Tea containers buried in Han-dynasty tombs.

● **59BC:** Wang Bao writes the first known book about tea.

● **AD600:** Chinese tea culture in full swing. Tea introduced to Japan by Buddhist monks.

● **AD760:** Lu Yu writes his seminal tea book, The Classic of Tea.

● **1658:** First documented reference to tea being drunk in Britain.

● **1839:** British tea production begins in India.

TASTING

Using the Chinese tea-steeping method known as *gong fu* makes tea drinking so much more pleasurable. You'll need a *gaiwan* (although a very small teapot will do), a strainer, a spouted cup or tea jug, and egg-cup sized teacups. Put two teaspoons of tea leaves into your *gaiwan* then pour in heated water. Don't drink this first steeping; this is for rinsing the tea leaves and your teaware. Repeat, but this time pour the steeped tea through the strainer into your tea jug. Drain all the tea from your *gaiwan* to prevent the leaves from stewing before the next steeping. Then pour your tea from the jug into each teacup. You can repeat these steepings 5–10 times, which makes even more expensive teas extremely economical.

WHITE
The purest of all teas. Perfect for moments of quiet reflection.

● Looks... lighter than green tea, with a silvery tinge.

● Tastes... delicately grassy.

● Perfect serving? Use the gong fu method. Water temperature: 85ºC. Steeping time: 5–10 seconds. Number of steepings: 5–6

OOLONG
Wide range of varieties and flavours, but most are rich and fruity.

● Looks... darker than green, lighter than black. Leaves often rolled into balls, which unfurl when steeped.

● Tastes... wonderfully fragrant, with a sweet creaminess and a lingering, fruity aftertaste.

● Perfect serving? Same as green, but with hotter water (95ºC) and longer steeping times (10–20 seconds).

GREEN
More caffeine than other teas. Ideal for a morning pick-me-up.

● Looks... olive green in colour. Sometimes the leaves are flattened.

● Tastes... grassier than white tea, with some toasted nuttiness.

● Perfect serving? Same as white, but with a lower water temperature (80ºC).

DID YOU KNOW?
● Most tea bags contain nothing but 'fannings' or 'dust'; tiny broken pieces of tea leaves that are left over after higher grades of tea are gathered to be sold.

BLACK
Full of rich, complex flavours which are lost if mixed with milk or sugar.

● Looks... darker and browner than most oolongs.

● Tastes... more earthy than grassy, with malty tones.

● Perfect serving? Use the gong fu method. Water temperature: 95ºC. Steeping time: 10 seconds. Number of steepings: 8–9

POST-FERMENTED
The connoisseur's choice. Best-known variety is pu'erh, which, like a fine wine, gets better with age.

● Looks... like a brick made of tea, after being machine-pressed.

● Tastes... extremely earthy, with a deep, long-lasting maltiness.

● Perfect serving? Steep in a small yixing teapot for 5–10 seconds per steeping. Water temperature: 95ºC. **Number of steepings: 15–20.**

ORIGINS

The name literally means
'pulled tea' – a reference to the
ritual of preparation. Before the
colonial period, tea in Malaysia
and Indonesia was mainly green,
but migrant workers from India
imported the tradition of black
tea served with milk. By luck,
their arrival coincided with the
invention of sweet condensed
milk, transforming second-rate
tea into something altogether
new and spectacular.

MALAYSIA & INDONESIA

TEH TARIK

SERVES 4

You haven't arrived in South East Asia until you've drunk a mug of *teh tarik* – a strongly steeped colonial cuppa served with a generous spoonful of sticky condensed milk. As chai is to India, *teh tarik* is to Southeast Asia.

YOU'LL NEED

1l (32fl oz) water

4 heaped tbs broken black tea leaves

4 generous tbs condensed milk

TASTING NOTES

Teh tarik originated with the Mamak (Indian Tamil) community, and Mamak food stalls are still the best place to enjoy the glorious theatre of its preparation. The 'pulling' of teh tarik is an art form – anything less than a metre between the two jugs that the tea is poured between would be considered amateur. Virtuoso tea-makers can pour two cups simultaneously, even sideways, while spinning backwards, sloshing the drink from one vessel to the next to achieve the perfect flavour, sweetness and consistency. Miraculously, not a drop is spilled.

● *by Joe Bindloss*

METHOD

1 Boil the water.

2 Place a sackcloth strainer in a large heatproof container.

3 Put the tea leaves in the strainer.

4 Pour over the boiling water.

5 Steep the tea leaves for at least 10 minutes, until the tea is dark and strongly brewed.

6 To make the first cup of tea, pour one cup of the steeped tea into a metal jug.

7 Stir in one generous tablespoon of condensed milk.

8 Start the pulling ritual. You will need another metal jug. The trick is to pour the mixture back and forth between the two jugs to generate the required foam and aeration. Start and end each pour with the two vessels close together, but hold them as far apart as you dare for the middle part of each pour. Six pours should be the minimum. This is your chance to be a showman, so don't be afraid to throw in a few stunt moves.

9 When the *teh tarik* is definitely 'pulled', pour it into a pre-warmed glass mug and serve it immediately.

10 Repeat the process with the remaining steeped tea and condensed milk.

ORIGINS

The beverage is a marriage between South East Asian coffee and 'pantyhose milk tea', the poor man's English tea. The latter, served at street stalls and *cha chaan tengs* (tea cafes), is brewed with eggshells for silkiness, and filtered through a cloth that hangs like a stocking. One day, an operator steeped in Chinese wisdom wondered, 'Tea has cool energy – yin; coffee has hot energy – yang. Why not combine the two?' Thus *yuan yang* was born. It's doused with creamy calorie-packed milk for the benefit of labourers.

HONG KONG

YUAN YANG

SERVES 4–6

A heady concoction of tea and coffee, with generous lashings of evaporated milk, *yuan yang* is an invigorating mid-morning drink and a bitter-sweet reminder of Hong Kong's colonial past.

YOU'LL NEED

360ml (12fl oz) water
1 tbs bold Ceylon tea leaves
1 tbs *Pu'erh* tea leaves
240ml (8fl oz) evaporated milk
120ml (4fl oz) extra-strong
    filtered robusta coffee
a little extra evaporated milk
sugar, to taste

TASTING NOTES

Yuan yang with milk is tan and opaque. The coffee's smoky bitterness cuts through the milk and sugar. Your taste buds are soon washed over by notes of spice and chocolate – that's the tea, with the rich and bold Ceylon tempered by the deep and woodsy insinuations of the *Pu'erh*. Then comes the sweet aftertaste, subtle and complex. If you want to make chilled *yuan yang*, leave the drink to cool, then chill it and serve it over ice.

● *by Piera Chan*

METHOD

1 Boil the water.

2 Put the tea leaves into a teapot.

3 Pour the boiling water over the tea leaves.

4 Leave the tea to steep for 7 minutes. Cover pot with a tea cosy if necessary.

5 (Optional) If you like your beverage very hot, place the milk in a heatproof bowl set over a pan of simmering water.

6 Stir the milk frequently, until bubbles form around the edge and steam begins to rise from the milk.

7 Remove the milk from the heat.

8 Fill a cup with tea to three-fifths full.

9 Add a fifth of a cup of coffee (so the golden ration of three parts tea and one part coffee is achieved).

10 Fill the rest of the cup with hot or cold evaporated milk. If you don't take milk, adjust the quantities of tea and coffee accordingly, maintaining the golden ratio.

11 Stir in sugar, to taste.

GLOSSARY

agave A succulent plant with rosettes of narrow spiny leaves and tall flower spikes, native to the southern US and tropical America, cultivated for their fibre and sap or for ornament.

aguardiente A generic term for strong alcoholic beverages that contain between 29% and 60% alcohol by volume. In Latin, the word is a combination of 'water' and 'fiery'. It was coined as the term for distilled spirits using whatever ingredients were available locally.

Angostura bitters A concentrated bitter or tonic, first made in Angostura obtained from a South American tree.

Benedictine A French liqueur based on brandy, originally made by Benedictine monks in France.

cachaça A Brazilian liquor distilled from sugar cane. The major difference between the Brazilian cachaça and Caribbean rum is that rum is usually made from molasses, while cachaça is made from fresh sugarcane juice that is fermented and distilled, producing two very different tastes.

campari An Italian pinkish aperitif flavoured with bitters, produced by the Alfredo Camari Group. It is coloured with cochineal, often mixed with soda water or orange juice, obtained from the infusion of herbs and fruit (included chinotto and cascarilla).

grenadine A commonly used sweet syrup made in France from pomegranates, characterised by its deep red colour and a flavour that is both tart and sweet. (See page 185 for the recipe).

Herbsaint Anise-flavoured liquor, originally used as a substitute for absinthe during the Prohibition. Originally made in New Orleans and currently produced by the Sazerac Company.

koji Yeast made from cooked rice or soya used to initiate fermentation of a mixture of soybeans and wheat to produce sake, soy sauce and miso.

marcha Spanish slang for 'to go out drinking'.

pétillant French term for slightly sparkling wine.

Peychaud's Bitters A bitter distributed by the Sazerac Company, developed in 1838 by Antoine Amédée Peychaud, a Creole apothecary who moved to New Orleans. He used a secret family recipe which consisted of mixing bitter with brandy and absinthe to create the first Sazerac.

simple syrup A liquefied form of sugar that is thick and sweet, commonly used to sweeten cocktails, iced drinks and soft drinks. It is much easier to blend into cold beverages than regular sugar. (To prepare a simple syrup,

combine equal volumes of water and sugar in a small saucepan. Heat over a medium heat, and stir until sugar dissolves. Cool. This will keep refrigerated for at least a month.)

Tabasco sauce A pungent sauce made from the fruit of a capsicum pepper, first produced in 1868 by Edmund McIlhenny, an American businessman and manufacturer.

tapioca pearls Tapioca is a starch extracted from cassava root native to South America and the Caribbean, but grown worldwide today. Tapioca pearls are produced by passing the moist starch through a sieve under pressure. Used in drinks, they provide a chewy contrast to the sweetness and texture of the liquid. Large pearls are preferred for use in drinks.

terroir The complete natural environment in which a particular wine is produced, including factors such as the soil, topography and climate that affect the characteristics, tastes and flavours of the wine.

Worcestershire sauce An English bottled sauce from the 19th century, it is a fermented liquid condiment of a complex mixture including tamarind extract, barley malt vinegar, spirit vinegar, molasses, sugar, salt, anchovies, shallots, onions and garlic.

AUTHORS

VICTORIA MOORE is a drink writer and flavour-obsessive with a particular interest in the psychology of smell and taste. As well as hosting wine tasting classes, holidays and dinners, she writes an award-winning wine column for the *Daily Telegraph* and runs her own website, howtodrink.co.uk. Her new book, *The Wine Dine Dictionary*, will be published by Granta in 2017.

Kate Armstrong Street-food connoisseur and lover of all things sweet. Capable chef. Global taste buds. Stomach of steel. Nothing – except oysters – is off her menu.

Mark Beales, who has lived in Thailand since 2004, has helped write more than a dozen Lonely Planet books. For more, visit www.markbeales.com.

Sarah Bennett co-writes Lonely Planet's New Zealand guidebooks. See her swing from the chandelier on Instagram @ TeamBenter.

Joe Bindloss is Lonely Planet's destination editor for the Indian subcontinent; he's a dyed-in-the-wool foodie and former food critic.

Celeste Brash is a contributor to The World as a Kitchen, writer of food and drinks sections for Lonely Planet and erstwhile professional chef.

Joshua Samuel Brown has written for Lonely Planet since 2007, likes his egg creams Manhattan style and is a true coffee snob. Follow him on twitter @josambro.

Piera Chen is a travel addict, sometime poet, and author of Lonely Planet books on Hong Kong and China.

Lucy Corne has written two books on the South African beer scene and blogs at www. brewmistress.co.za. She is yet to meet an IPA that she doesn't like.

Helen Elfer is a Destination Editor at Lonely Planet. She loves bringing bottles of obscure liquor back from holidays and can mix a mean martini (gin, dry, two olives, thanks).

Bridget Gleeson writes for Lonely Planet's South America guides. She's equally fond of the Brazilian caipirinha and the pisco sours of Peru and Chile.

Ben Handicott once published travel pictorial and reference books for a living, now dreams about, writes about and sometimes even does, travel. Eats and drinks too.

Carolyn B. Heller is a Vancouver-based travel and food writer who has sipped and supped her way across five continents.

Anita Isalska is a travel writer with an unquenchable thirst for cocktails, wine trails and excellent coffee. Find more of her work on anitaisalska.com.

Adam Karlin bellies up to dive bars and lounges around the world as a Lonely Planet author, and increases his tolerance by living in New Orleans.

Catherine Le Nevez is a Lonely Planet author primarily based (wanderlust aside) in foodie mecca Paris; Doctor of Creative Arts in Writing; Bloody Mary devotee.

Alex Leviton has been writing for Lonely Planet since 2002, around the time she developed her milkshake habit. She shares recipes and blogs about minimalism, the meaning of life, and travel at likeahouse.com.

Daniel McCrohan is a British travel writer based in Beijing. He wrote the section on tea, a drink he has grown fascinated by since moving to China more than a decade ago. His favourite brew? Alishan oolong.

From sopi in Indonesia to mead balsam in Lithuania, Hugh McNaughton is usually straight into the local tipple when on the road for Lonely Planet. Not much beats a West-country cider on a hot day, he's found.

Karyn Noble is a senior editor in Lonely Planet's London office and a freelance writer specialising in gourmet food and luxury travel. Apart from the enjoyable aspects of drinks research for this book, she trampled Hampshire's prickly blackthorn bushes, emerging scratched, bleeding, but triumphant, with a basket of sloes. She'd do it again if gin was the end result.

Zora O'Neill has been writing for Lonely Planet since 2005; her guidebook beats have included Mexico, Egypt and Spain. She lives in Queens, New York, where she can eat food from dozens of countries in a single day. Find her travel stories at www.rovinggastronome.com.

Stephanie Ong is an Australian writer based in Milan, Italy. When she's not writing for Lonely Planet, Expedia and Le Cool Publishing, she's eating well and complaining about tax – like every good Italian.

Lorna Parkes is a destination editor at Lonely Planet HQ and considers no trip complete without a thorough investigation of the local food and drink scene wherever she travels.

Matt Phillips loves quenching his thirst, and given he's actively explored dozens of rather toasty countries for Lonely Planet, he knows his beverages.

Lonely Planet author Josephine Quintero has had 20-plus years of living near the beach (bars) in southern Spain to perfect her sangria recipe.

Helen Ranger writes for Lonely Planet's Morocco, South Africa and Madagascar guidebooks and has contributed to several LP foodie books. Travel and food – a sublime combination!

Kevin Raub lives in Brazil and writes for Lonely Planet guides throughout North/South America, the Caribbean and India. He tries not to drink too many caipirinhas on deadline. His website is www.kevinraub.net.

Travel journalist and Lonely Planet Destination Editor Sarah Reid has happily quaffed her way around more than 80 countries to date.

Lee Slater co-writes Lonely Planet's New Zealand guidebooks. See him carousing on Instagram @TeamBenter.

Luna Soo is a part-time writer and full-time drinker who's exploring the world one bar at a time. She writes about cocktails at fiftytwococktails.com

Regis St. Louis has written about unique libations and other travel-related matters in dozens of Lonely Planet guides. Follow him on twitter at @regis_st_louis.

Phillip Tang has lived in Mexico for the last few years, taste-testing drinks for the Lonely Planet Mexico and Peru guides, among others. Check out the photos, tweets, gifs and articles of his research through philliptang.co.uk.

Caroline Veldhuis contributes to LP travel/culture books, and is a lifelong vegetarian known to fill up on drinks and desserts.

When not deskbound in LP's Melbourne office, Steve Waters can usually be found knee deep in bog in South-West Tasmania.

INDEX

The World's Best Drinks

March 2016
Published by Lonely Planet Publications Pty Ltd
ABN 36 005 607 983
90 Maribyrnong St, Footscray,
Victoria, 3011, Australia
www.lonelyplanet.com
10 9 8 7 6 5 4 3 2 1

Printed in China
ISBN 978 1 76034 061 2
© Lonely Planet 2016
© photographers as indicated 2016

Foreword written by Victoria Moore

Managing Director, Publishing Piers Pickard
Associate Publisher Robin Barton
Commissioning Editor Jessica Cole
Art Director Daniel Di Paolo
Layout Designer and Illustrator Hayley Warnham
Cover Illustration by Muti - Folio Art
Editors Kate Turvey, Christina Webb
Pre-Press Production Nigel Longuet
Print Production Larissa Frost

Written by Kate Armstrong, Mark Beales, Sarah
Bennett, Joe Bindloss, Celeste Brash, Joshua
Samuel Brown, Piera Chen, Lucy Corne, Helen Elfer,
Bridget Gleeson, Ben Handicott, Carolyn B. Heller,
Anita Isalska, Adam Karlin, Catherine Le Nevez, Alex
Leviton, Daniel McCrohan, Hugh McNaughton,
Karyn Noble, Zora O'Neill, Stephanie Ong,
Lorna Parkes, Matt Phillips, Josephine Quintero,
Helen Ranger, Kevin Raub, Sarah Reid, Lee Slater,
Luna Soo, Regis St. Louis, Phillip Tang,
Caroline Veldhuis, Steve Waters

With thanks to Renata Bartik, Carolina Esteves and
the team at Cubana (www.cubana.co.uk).
Luke Shackleton and mixologists Jack Dobson and
Zane McRae at the City of London Distillery
(www.cityoflondondistillery.com).

Lonely Planet Offices

Australia
Level 2 & 3, 551 Swanston Street,
Carlton 3053, Victoria
Phone 03 8379 8000 Fax 03 8379 8111
Email talk2us@lonelyplanet.com.au

USA
150 Linden St, Oakland, CA 94607
Phone 510 250 6400 Toll free 800 275 8555
Fax 510 893 8572
Email info@lonelyplanet.com

Europe
240 Blackfriars Road, London, SE1 8NW
Phone 020 3771 5100 Fax 020 3771 5101
Email go@lonelyplanet.co.uk

MIX
Paper from
responsible sources
FSC
www.fsc.org   FSC™ C021741